SO YOU THINK YOU KNOW
ROALD DAHL?

SO YOU THINK YOU KNOW

ROALD DAHL?

Clive Gifford

Hodder
Children's
Books

a division of Hodder Headline Limited

This book is not affiliated with or endorsed by Roald Dahl or
publishers of his books. It does not imply or claim any rights
to the characters or creations.

© Hodder Children's Books 2004

Published in Great Britain in 2004
by Hodder Children's Books

Editor: Vic Parker
Design by Fiona Webb
Cover design: Hodder Children's Books

The right of Clive Gifford to be identified as the author of the work has been
asserted by him in accordance with the Copyright, Designs and Patents Act
1988.

10 9 8 7 6 5 4 3 2

ISBN: 0340884487

Printed by Bookmarque Ltd, Croydon, Surrey

The paper and board used in this paperback by Hodder Children's Books are
natural recyclable products made from wood grown in sustainable forests.
The manufacturing processes conform to the environmental regulations of the
country of origin.

Hodder Children's Books
a division of Hodder Headline Limited
338 Euston Road
London NW1 3BH

CONTENTS

INTRODUCTION

So you think you know all about Roald Dahl's extraordinary books? Reckon you can remember all his weird and wonderful characters and the wild adventures they had? Think you're an expert on the amazing life of the man behind the stories?

Well, this book contains more than 1,000 questions to put you to the test. Most will quiz you on Roald Dahl's tales for children and young adults, but there's also a sprinkling of questions about the author himself. Many of the questions are more slippery than fantastic Mr Fox, others are tougher than the skin of a leathery old witch. Good luck!

ECCENTRICALLY EASY QUESTIONS

1   What is the name of the boy who won a prize to go to a chocolate factory?

2   Which book features a little girl with amazing powers involving reading, maths and moving objects: *The Witches*, *Matilda* or *The BFG*?

3   What does BFG stand for: Blue Furry Gryphon, Big Friendly Giant or Brown Fairy Goblin?

4   Was Roald Dahl a man or a woman?

5   In which book do you first read about magical chocolates and Oompa-Loompas?

6   What is the name of the book about a giant-sized creature with lots of teeth who plots how to eat children?

7   In *The Twits*, is the Roly-Poly creature a bird, a tiger or a hippo?

8   Which book features a small boy and an enormous piece of fruit?

9   What is the name of the chocolate factory owner in *Charlie and the Chocolate Factory*?

10 What is the title of the collection of Dahl's poems which includes *Hot and Cold* and *Mary, Mary* – is it: *Poem Puddles*, *Rhyme Stew* or *Pages of Poems*?

11 Which country did Roald Dahl's parents come from: Scotland, Norway or Germany?

12 Which book features lots of tiny people who live in a forest and are threatened by a smoke-belching monster: *The Twits*, *The Minpins* or *The Witches*?

13 In the 1971 film of *Charlie and the Chocolate Factory*, who played Willy Wonka: Gene Wilder, Jude Law or Gene Hackman?

14 Some of Roald Dahl's scary tales were turned into a television show. What was its full title?

15 In which book do a boy and his grandmother stay in a hotel in Bournemouth: *The Witches*, *The Minpins* or *The BFG*?

16 Which book features families of underground animals who are threatened by farmers digging up the land: *The BFG*, *Fantastic Mr Fox* or *The Minpins*?

17 Can you name Roald Dahl's first cookbook, which features recipes inspired by his stories?

18 In which country was Roald Dahl born and brought up: England, Scotland, Wales or Norway?

19 What is the name of the little girl in *The BFG*: Sheila, Sophie, Sandra or Samantha?

20 In *The Witches*, which of the boy's parents are dead: his mother, his father, or both his mother and father?

21 In *The BFG*, what is the name of the biggest creature of all: Fleshlumpeater, the BFG or Childcruncher?

22 In *Charlie and the Chocolate Factory*, is Charlie: an only child, an orphan or one of three brothers?

23 What sort of creatures accompany James on his adventures with the giant peach?

24 In *The Giraffe and the Pelly and Me*, what is the only thing that Geraneous Giraffes can eat: certain flowers, one type of grass or chocolate biscuits?

25 Roald Dahl served in which major war: the Vietnam War, World War I or World War II?

26 In *The Witches*, what does the magic Formula 86 turn children into?

27 In *The BFG*, which queen did the BFG get to meet?

28 Roald Dahl wrote most of his stories in: a treehouse, a garden shed, a French farmhouse or a castle turret?

29 In which book do hoardes of witches stay in a hotel by the sea?

30 Which book tells the tale of four monkeys and some birds getting their own back on a horrible couple: *The Minpins, The Twits* or *The Witches*?

31 What is the name of the follow-up to *Charlie and the Chocolate Factory*?

32 Roald Dahl co-invented a type of medical valve used to drain fluid from the brain: true or false?

33 Which creature's name is spelt out in the letters of Roald Dahl's book, *Esio Trot*?

34 Which book features a grandmother who grows much taller than a house: *Charlie and the Great Glass Elevator, George's Marvellous Medicine* or *Matilda*?

35 Which book features a kind man who gets his words in a muddle: *The Twits*, *The Vicar of Nibbleswicke* or *George's Marvellous Medicine*?

36 In *Rhyme Stew*, who did the tortoise bet he could win a race with?

37 What colour are the tickets, hidden inside chocolate bars, which let you enter Willy Wonka's magical chocolate factory?

38 Which book features a whole village of people interested in poaching pheasants?

39 In which book would you find poems about Aladdin, Dick Whittington and Hansel and Gretel?

40 Roald Dahl wrote the screenplay to a popular children's film which features a magical flying car. Can you name it?

41 In which book do a boy and some giant insects cross the Atlantic Ocean?

42 In *The Enormous Crocodile*, what sort of animal is Trunky?

43 Which book ends with the characters visiting the President of the United States?

44 Which book features lots of giants who eat people and one who doesn't?

45 In *Charlie and the Great Glass Elevator*, where is the Space Hotel: in space, on the south coast of England or in Norway?

46 In *Matilda*, which of these women is evil: the grandmother, the school headmistress or the class teacher?

47 In which book can you find poems titled *The Cow*, *The Porcupine* and *The Crocodile*?

48 When Roald Dahl was at school, he and his classmates tested out the latest chocolate inventions from Cadbury's: true or false?

49 How many Roald Dahl books feature Willy Wonka?

50 In which book can you find two horrible aunts, a giant green grasshopper and a giant centipede?

MADCAP &
MUDDLESOME
MEDIUM QUESTIONS

1 In *James and the Giant Peach*, what creature was on the ceiling of the peach stone and lit up the room?

2 Dahl fought in World War II as: a commando, a member of the Resistance, a fighter pilot or a tank commander?

3 In *James and the Giant Peach*, who made too much noise so that the Cloud-Men spotted the giant peach: James, the grasshopper or the centipede?

4 In *The Witches*, the mouse swings like a trapeze artist using which part of its body?

5 The BFG was turned into a giant by a witch almost 100 years ago: true or false?

6 In *Charlie and the Chocolate Factory*, which of Charlie's grandparents bought him a second chocolate bar?

7   In *James and the Giant Peach*, the tiny stones or crystals which caused the peach and the insects to grow in size were what colour?

8   Which one of the following is not a recipe in *Revolting Recipes*: Stink Bugs' Eggs, Krokan Ice-Cream or Candy Insects?

9   Which one of the following is not a creature mentioned in *The Minpins*: Snozzwangers, Clawsizzlers or Hornswogglers?

10 In *Charlie and the Chocolate Factory*, is Mr Bucket: a quiet shy man, a loud cheerful man or a loud angry man?

11 Who took George's Medicine Number Four and shrank without trace?

12 In Roald Dahl's poem *The Crocodile*, what is the name of the crocodile?

13 In *Matilda*, which schoolgirl is tiny, has dark hair and brown eyes, and becomes a friend of Matilda's?

14 In *The Giraffe and the Pelly and Me*, how many policemen arrived to capture the burglar?

15 In *The Witches*, what time do the witches plan to have dinner at the hotel?

16   In *Danny The Champion of the World*, what
     did Danny and his father do to the raisins before
     filling them with sleeping-pill powder?

17   How tall is the BFG: 24 feet, 36 feet, 50 feet
     or 64 feet?

18   In *The Witches*, where did the Grand High Witch
     hide her bottles of magic formula?

19   In *The Giraffe and the Pelly and Me*, which one
     of these sweets does not come from the Land of
     the Midnight Sun: Liplickers, Gobwangles or
     Plushnuggets?

20   In *Danny The Champion of the World*, the
     shooting party was full of Lords and Dukes
     on which day of the week?

21   In *Charlie and the Chocolate Factory*, Charlie
     and his family had double helpings of cabbage
     and potatoes on which day of the week?

22   Two ravens covered which part of Mr and Mrs
     Twit with the world's strongest glue?

23   In *George's Marvellous Medicine*, was George's
     father: a policeman, a chemist, a farmer or a
     librarian?

24 How old was Matilda when she first attended school: four and a half, five and a half, six and a half or seven and a half?

25 What was the Enormous Crocodile's favourite food: biscuits, children, manburgers or cherry pie?

26 In *James and the Giant Peach*, which creature was used as bait to entice the seagulls?

27 In which book does a little girl go to Crunchem Hall Primary School?

28 In *Matilda*, what creature did Lavender slip into Miss Trunchbull's water jug?

29 In *Fantastic Mr Fox*, what does Farmer Bean grow: apples, potatoes, cherries or turnips?

30 In *Charlie and the Chocolate Factory*, what coin did Charlie find in the snow?

31 In *The Witches*, when Bruno and the boy are first spotted by the chambermaid, do they hide in: a pair of shoes, a pair of trousers or a small cardboard box?

32 In *Danny The Champion of the World*, how many gamekeepers always patrol Hazell's Wood: one, three or five?

33 What did James discover on the side of the giant peach at night: a sign, a tunnel or a secret code?

34 In *The Witches*, the Grand High Witch says that her Delayed Action Mouse-Maker formula will work when children are arriving where?

35 In *Charlie and the Great Glass Elevator*, the rope that towed the spacecraft was made of: superstrong candyfloss, reinscorched steel, cats' hairs or titanium?

36 In *Charlie and the Great Glass Elevator*, after Grandma Georgina had taken the growing-younger pills, how old did Willy Wonka say she had become?

37 Matilda tipped over the glass of water using what part of her body?

38 In *James and the Giant Peach*, who gave James a white bag containing what he said was lots of crocodile tongues?

39 In *The Witches*, the boy entered the hotel ballroom while trying to train what sort of creatures?

40 Do Oompa-Loompas come up to the height of a normal person's ankle, knee or waist?

41 Where did Roald Dahl have a childhood hideaway: in a treehouse, in an old air raid shelter or in the attic of his house?

42 At the end of *James and the Giant Peach*, James's peach-stone house was situated in which New York park?

43 In *Charlie and the Chocolate Factory*, who says that breakfast cereals are made of pencil shavings?

44 In *Rhyme Stew*, what animal did Ali Baba see asleep in one of the posh hotel beds: a fox, a goat or a hippo?

45 At the start of *Esio Trot*, how long did it take for Alfie the tortoise to grow to double his size: five, 10, 20 or 30 years?

46 In *Matilda*, Hortensia put itching powder into whose gym knickers: Miss Plimsoll's, Miss Honey's or Miss Trunchbull's?

47 Matilda uses her willpower to tip something over Miss Trunchbull. What is it?

48 What does the giant named Bloodbottler call the BFG: weed, runt, puny, or shorty?

49 In *Matilda*, was Miss Honey's father called: Magnus, Marchwood or Manglethorpe?

50 In *The Minpins*, Little Billy rides what sort of bird?

QUIZ 2

1 In *The Ant-Eater* poem, what is the name of the unpleasant boy: George, Craig or Roy?

2 Matilda's father taught her to read with all the books in his library: true or false?

3 In *Danny The Champion of the World*, Danny's dad says there are three things you must have with roasted pheasant. Can you name any one of them?

4 Sophie and the BFG tried to save children from being eaten by heading at night to which city?

5 In 1952, Roald Dahl moved from England to which American city?

6 In *George's Marvellous Medicine*, when the chicken laid an egg, was it the size of: a coconut, a football or a beachball?

7   In *Dirty Beasts*, what building did Roy rush to after his aunt was eaten?

8   In *Matilda*, Mrs Wormwood used to go to Aylesbury every week to do what: go to the market, play bingo, visit her mother or play badminton?

9   In *The Witches*, the Grand High Witch tells the other witches that she plans to turn the boy into which sort of fish: a mackerel, a haddock, a guppy or a goldfish?

10   In *Matilda*, Miss Honey had to give Miss Trunchbull her salary for how many years?

11   The first article Roald Dahl ever sold told the true story of someone narrowly escaping death from which African creature?

12   In *Matilda*, which adult was very poor and had only boxes for furniture?

13   In *The Giraffe and the Pelly and Me*, which of these are sweets from Africa: Gumtwizzlers, Fizzwinkles or Frothblowers?

14   In *Dirty Beasts*, from which country did Roy's parents finally buy their son a giant ant-eater?

15   In *Esio Trot*, who worked part-time in a shop selling sweets and newspapers?

16   The grandma in *The Witches* was missing whch part of her body: a leg, a thumb, an ear or an arm?

17   In *The Witches*, the boy first encountered around 200 witches in what room of the hotel?

18   Roald Dahl had dinner with President Roosevelt at the White House during World War II: true or false?

19   In *Charlie and the Chocolate Factory*, who ignored Willy Wonka's warning, and grabbed and ate the stick of Three-Course Chewing Gum?

20   In *Matilda*, was Nigel Hicks's father: a doctor, a policeman, a dentist or a lawyer?

21   In *The Giraffe and the Pelly and Me*, is the Duke of Hampshire an expert on the animals of: Africa, Asia or Europe?

22   In *Esio Trot*, Mr Hoppy was advised to feed his tortoises on the leaves of which vegetable?

23   In *James and the Giant Peach*, who cut the stem holding the peach to the tree: the centipede, the grasshopper or the glow-worm?

24 In *Even More Revolting Recipes*, are Nishnobblers: a type of cake, a type of vegetable dish or a type of chocolate?

25 Roald Dahl had dinner with King George VI at Buckingham Palace during World War II: true or false?

26 In *Boy*, Roald Dahl says that the second school he attended was called: St Anne's, St Peter's or St Thomas's?

27 In *The Minpins*, many go into the forest but how many come out?

28 Do the people-eating giants in *The BFG* attack: at night, at day or on Christmas Eve?

29 Who was the first adult Matilda told about her magic powers?

30 What does the BFG call Charles Dickens by mistake?

31 In *James and the Giant Peach*, someone points out that they can eat some of the giant peach as food. Who is this?

32 In *Charlie and the Chocolate Factory*, how many rooms were there in Charlie's house?

33 Who provided the illustrations for many of Roald Dahl's books: Quentin Blake, Ronald Searle or Maurice Sendak?

34 In *Boy*, Roald Dahl says that when he was young, another boy told him that a certain type of sweet was made from rats' blood. Was this: sherbet, liquorice or aniseed balls?

35 How many teeth did the crocodile in *The Dentist and the Crocodile* have: one, 100 or 300?

36 In *Rhyme Stew*, after Ali Baba learned the magic door-opening words, which hotel did he go to?

37 What place did the Enormous Crocodile visit straight after the school playground: the tribal village, the local bank or the fairground?

38 In *The Magic Finger*, how old was the girl who lived on a farm?

39 In Willy Wonka's chocolate factory, the boat travelled through the big tunnel then entered which room?

40 After the Great Glass Elevator re-entered the Earth's atmosphere, what building did it crash into?

41 Roald Dahl's eldest daughter died at age seven after which illness: measles, mumps, pneumonia or whooping cough?

42 When Matilda was reading *Great Expectations* by Charles Dickens, was she: four, five, six or seven years of age?

43 In *The Giraffe and the Pelly and Me*, how many windows does the Duke's house have: 465, 677, 766 or 909?

44 When the grandma in *The Witches* is ill, a lady comes to the house to clean and cook for her. Is her name: Mrs Spring, Mrs Fall or Mrs Summer?

45 Which book features a bird, a monkey and a giraffe, who clean a Duke's house which has hundreds of windows?

46 In *The Witches*, whose room is directly above the Grand High Witch's: the boy's room, the grandma's room, or Bruno Jenkins's room?

47 In *Charlie and the Chocolate Factory*, how many children does Willy Wonka plan to invite into his factory?

48 In *Rhyme Stew*, what was the name of the boy who kissed a girl and gave her a cold?

49 In *James and the Giant Peach*, did the sharks:
    eat half of the peach, eat a quarter of the peach
    or barely damage the peach?

50 In which book does a man buy lots of tortoises to
    pretend that a lady's tortoise has grown bigger?

QUIZ 3

1 What is the name of the dark forest in
   The Minpins?

2 What sort of fruit was the Duke of Hampshire
   instructing his gardener to pick when the giraffe,
   the pelican and others arrived?

3 The BFG blew a nightmare into a giant called:
   Fleshlumpeater, Childchewer or Meatdripper?

4 In *Boy*, Roald Dahl said he got how many strokes
   of Mr Coombes's cane?

5 In *Matilda*, what was the name of the boy that
   Miss Trunchbull held in the air by his ears?

6 At Willy Wonka's chocolate factory, what was the
   name of the drink which lifted you into the air so
   you had to burp to get back down?

7   Which one of these is not a poem in *Dirty Beasts: The Scorpion, The Lobster* or *The Porcupine*?

8   The King of Arabia sent what type of creature to the BFG and to Sophie?

9   In *The Magic Finger*, which member of the Gregg family is upset that a giant duck is playing with his train set?

10   Which ocean did James and the insects fly over on the giant peach?

11   In *Danny The Champion of the World*, how many teachers were there at Danny's school: four, eight, 12 or 16?

12   The giant peach landed on which of these buildings: Buckingham Palace, the Empire State Building, Windsor Castle or the White House?

13   In *Dirty Beasts*, which creature reminds a boy of his Aunt Emily?

14   The girl in *The Magic Finger* makes a creature follow the Greggs around. What creature is this?

15   In *The Magic Finger*, who suggests that the Gregg family eats wormburgers?

16   Who warned the schoolchildren about the Enormous Crocodile in their playground: the Roly-Poly Bird, Muggle-Wump or Trunky?

17   Which meal does the Queen of England ask her servants to make for Sophie and the BFG: breakfast, lunch, dinner or supper?

18   In *James and the Giant Peach*, which two insects weave enough rope to enable James's plan to escape from the sharks?

19   Where did the giant peach grow: on the lowest tree branch, on the highest tree branch or straight out of the ground?

20   In *Rhyme Stew*, who first ate at Mr Roach's cabbage patch: the tortoise, the rat or the hare?

21   In *Dirty Beasts*, which creature realised that the meaning of its life was to be fattened so that he could be eaten?

22   In *Danny The Champion of the World*, Danny helped to get his father out of the pit by using what item in the old Baby Austin car?

23   In *George's Marvellous Medicine*, what was the name of George's pony: Trigger, Jack Frost, White Lightning or Dapple?

24 What was the name of Roald Dahl's mother: Sofie, Patricia, Mari or Janice?

25 In *Charlie and the Great Glass Elevator*, what happens if you take a drop of Vita-Wonk: you grow younger, you grow fatter, you grow older, you grow thinner?

26 After George boiled the medicine in the saucepan, what colour did it become?

27 In *The BFG*, who mixed around 50 dreams together in order to save English children being eaten by giants?

28 In *George's Marvellous Medicine*, what colour was the bottle of sheepdip?

29 When a creature took some of George's Medicine Number Three, what part of its body grew?

30 What is the name of the headmistress in *Matilda*?

31 In *The Giraffe and the Pelly and Me*, from which country do Giant Wangdoodle sweets come from: USA, Australia, Peru or Albania?

32 In *Charlie and the Great Glass Elevator*, who inside the Space Hotel spoke to the President of the United States in a made-up language?

33 In *Charlie and the Chocolate Factory*, who won't dive into the river to save his son because he is wearing his best suit: Mr Salt, Mr Gloop or Mr Teavee?

34 In *Boy*, what was said to give you sharp, pointed teeth: ratitis, rabbititus or mousemonia?

35 Which creature inside the peach stone tells James and the other insects to go to bed: the grasshopper, the silkworm or the spider?

36 In *Danny The Champion of the World*, what name did Danny give the wooden go-kart his father made for him: Soapo, Whizzo, Speedo or Whamo?

37 In *Boy*, Roald Dahl said that from the ages of seven to nine he went to which school: Cardiff, Llandaff or St David's?

38 *Hornets Stewed in Tar* is a recipe inspired by which Roald Dahl storybook?

39 Which book sees a family promise not to hunt wild animals after some of the wild animals threaten them with guns?

40 In *The Magic Finger*, who suggests first that the Greggs should build a nest?

41 How did the new Vicar of Nibbleswicke address the first member of his parish that he met: Miss Fool, Miss Twerp or Miss Understanding?

42 In *The Witches*, what was the boy building in the conker tree when he met his first witch?

43 In *Matilda*, how old was Miss Honey when her father died: five, 12, 15 or 20?

44 In *Danny The Champion of the World*, how old was Danny when he drove the old Baby Austin car to Hazell Wood: nine, 11, or 13 years old?

45 In *Danny The Champion of the World*, which one of the following birds does not make its nest on the ground: nightingale, robin, grouse, skylark?

46 How old was Roald Dahl when he was sent to boarding school?

47 Who swings the Enormous Crocodile around so fast that he crashes into the sun?

48 How many insects did James find inside the giant peach's stone: three, five, seven or nine?

49 Which character in *Charlie and the Chocolate Factory* wears grey gloves and carries a cane?

50 In *Esio Trot*, how many floors below Mr Hoppy does Mrs Silver live?

QUIZ 4

1 In the poem *The Tortoise and the Hare*, was the rat brilliant at: engineering, mathematics or astronomy?

2 What colour are Willy Wonka's trousers?

3 In the poem *A Little Nut Tree* from *Rhyme Stew*, what were the three words that the nut tree said to the little girl?

4 Roald Dahl used to drive his children to school wearing his nightshirt and slippers: true or false?

5 Can you name the two of the three worms James found inside the giant peach?

6 Which book contains a recipe for Wonka's Whipple-Scrumptious Fudgemallow Delight?

7 Willy Wonka shows Charlie and the other Golden Ticket winners some Three-Course Chewing Gum. Can you name any one of the courses?

8   In *Revolting Recipes*, there is a recipe for
    Lickable Wallpaper for Nurseries: true or false?

9   In *The Giraffe and the Pelly and Me*, the
    burglar armed with a pistol stole jewels from
    whose bedroom?

10 The Enormous Crocodile posed as what sort
    of tree, in order to catch and eat a child?

11 In *James and the Giant Peach*, a Cloud-Man
    covered the centipede in paint of which colour?

12 When the Enormous Crocodile met the monkey,
    the monkey was eating what food from trees?

13 In *Danny The Champion of the World*, Danny's
    father visits Captain Lancaster to beat him up:
    true or false?

14 In *The Witches*, who made the mouse a tiny
    toothbrush out of a matchstick?

15 Which of the following was Roald Dahl's first
    famous children's book: *The BFG*, *Charlie
    and the Chocolate Factory* or *James and the
    Giant Peach*?

16 At the end of *Charlie and the Great Glass
    Elevator*, Charlie and his family are invited to
    the house of which world leader?

17   In which book can you find a Reverend who suffered from Dyslexia as a child?

18   Mr and Mrs Bucket enjoyed their ride into space in the Great Glass Elevator: true or false?

19   What creature did the Enormous Crocodile bite on the leg as it was eating leaves?

20   In *The BFG*, what is the name of the nastiest giant of all: Fleshlumpeating Giant, Bloodbottler Giant or Bonecrushing Giant?

21   Roald Dahl wrote a young person's guide on: railway safety, kitchen safety or road safety?

22   What is the first name of Matilda's father: Michael, Harry or George?

23   At the end of *Matilda*, Matilda's mum and dad are suddenly moving to which country?

24   In *Rhyme Stew*, how many yen did the man offer Aladdin to get the magic lamp: 10 yen, 20 yen, 50 yen or 100 yen?

25   In *The Witches*, in what room in the hotel does the boy plan to add the magic formula to the witches' meals?

26 In *Charlie and the Great Glass Elevator*, how old did Grandma Georgina become when she was aged by Willy Wonka: 241, 358, 379 or 426?

27 In *Dirty Beasts*, how often did Roy the spoilt boy get two pairs of shoes: every day, every week or every month?

28 In *Boy*, Roald Dahl says that a member of his family died when he was three years old. Was it: his brother, his mother or his father?

29 What does Roald Dahl say in *Boy* was the name of the woman who ran the sweet shop at Llandaff School?

30 In *Fantastic Mr Fox*, which of the farmers came up with the idea of digging the foxes out with shovels?

31 After the shovels, what did the farmers use next to try to dig out fantastic Mr Fox?

32 Which child in *Charlie and the Chocolate Factory* gets shrunk by television?

33 When the Enormous Crocodile was on the fairground ride, which two of the following did it stand between: a lion, a fire engine, a dragon, a train?

34   In *Danny The Champion of the World*, Doc Spencer was given two pheasants: true or false?

35   According to Willy Wonka, Vermicious Knids live on what planet: Venus, Vermes, Andros Seven or Hermes?

36   What times table were Matilda's class to be tested on by the headmistress?

37   *The Giraffe and the Pelly and Me*, what sort of shop had The Grubber been in the past: a shoe shop, a cleaning shop, a sweet shop or a café?

38   In *Danny The Champion of the World*, which one of the staff at Danny's school was always drinking gin: Captain Lancaster, Mr Snoddy or Mr Corrado?

39   In *Charlie and the Great Glass Elevator*, what was the new vitamin Willy Wonka invented which made people feel younger?

40   In *Boy*, what did Roald Dahl say happened to the sweet shop the day after the children put a dead mouse in a sweet jar?

41   Which book features the recipe Pickled Spines of Porcupines: *James and the Giant Peach*, *Revolting Recipes* or *Even More Revolting Recipes*?

42 What were the first three words James heard spoken by the insects inside the giant peach: 'Look who's here', 'Hello there, James', or 'Run away, child'?

43 In *James and the Giant Peach*, what creature (which had escaped from London Zoo) had eaten James's parents?

44 According to *Charlie and the Great Glass Elevator*, who was the youngest of Charlie's grandparents?

45 George changed his Medicine Number Three into Medicine Number Four by adding two ingredients. Can you name either of them?

46 Was the temperature inside Willy Wonka's chocolate factory: freezing-cold, normal room temperature or very hot?

47 In *The Magic Finger*, which member of the Gregg family is upset that a giant duck is sleeping in his bed?

48 Which child in *Charlie and the Chocolate Factory* wore a silver mink coat: Violet Beauregarde, Mike Teavee or Veruca Salt?

49 People from which country in Britain taste fishy according to the giant in *The BFG*?

50   In *Even More Revolting Recipes*, plastic straws
     are used to help make: Spitsizzlers, Sherbet
     Slurpers or Devil's Drenchers?

QUIZ 5

1   In *The Witches*, is there a Secret Society of
    Witches in: 10 countries, 24 countries or all the
    countries of the world?

2   What was the name of the maid who brought the
    Queen her breakfast in *The BFG*: Mary, Constance,
    Emily or Hannah?

3   In *The Witches*, when the grandmother tried to
    give Mrs Jenkins her son back, was Mrs Jenkins:
    eating, swimming, knitting or reading?

4   What sort of hat did Willy Wonka wear: a top hat,
    a fez, a woolly hat or a chef's hat?

5   In *The Witches*, the grandmother, smoked cigars:
    true or false?

6   In *Revolting Recipes*, there is a recipe for making
    a half-a-metre wide giant peach dessert: true or
    false?

7 Which C.S. Lewis book did Matilda tell Miss Honey was her favourite book she had read so far?

8 The Tummyticklers recipe was inspired by which Roald Dahl book: *Boy, The BFG* or *The Giraffe and the Pelly and Me*?

9 In *Danny The Champion of the World*, how did police sergeant Samways arrive at the petrol filling station: on a bike, on foot, in a police car or in a police helicopter?

10 In *Rhyme Stew*, what type of creature ate Hansel and Gretel's trail of breadcrumbs: crows, sparrows, vultures or owls?

11 What was the name of Dahl's first published children's story: *The Gremlins, The Minpins, Charlie and the Chocolate Factory* or *The Twits*?

12 In *The BFG*, did Sophie: live with her parents, live with her grandmother or live in an orphanage?

13 Which Roald Dahl book would be reading if you learned of a horrid couple playing equally terrible tricks on each other, such as putting worms in spaghetti?

14 In Roald Dahl's *Mary, Mary* poem, what sort of home did Mary live in?

15 In *Charlie and the Chocolate Factory*, what creatures come from Loompaland?

16 The Enormous and the Notsobig One are what type of African animal?

17 In *Esio Trot*, which tortoise is too big to get inside Mrs Silver's tortoise house: tortoise number four, tortoise number eight or tortoise number 11?

18 In the poem *Hansel and Gretel*, what do Hansel and Gretel scatter on the ground to find their way back?

19 In *Fantastic Mr Fox*, what was the name of the chicken farmer?

20 In *The BFG*, who stuck a three-inch long pin into the ankle of Fleshlumpeater?

21 What New Zealand city sent Sophie and the BFG 100 pairs of boots each?

22 In *James and the Giant Peach*, which two creatures pulled the earthworm back down the tunnel every time a bird appeared?

23   In *The Giraffe and the Pelly and Me*, who offers rewards of special flowers for the giraffe, walnuts for the monkey, and salmon for the pelican?

24   In *Boy*, the headmaster of Roald Dahl's school later became: the Bishop of Chester, the head of the Metropolitan Police or a British Prime Minister?

25   Which foreign language did Roald Dahl learn to speak in his early twenties: French, Swahili, Japanese or German?

26   How much chocolate is needed to make one pill of Wonka-Vite: one pound, one kilo, one hundred pounds or one ton?

27   In *Dirty Beasts*, who did the giant ant-eater eat first?

28   Which military service did Dahl join at the beginning of World War II?

29   What part of the Roly-Poly Bird did the Enormous Crocodile manage to catch in his jaws?

30   What sort of vehicle was to take Willy Wonka, Charlie and his family to meet the President of the United States: Concorde, a black limousine, a helicopter or a speedboat?

31   How much did Dahl receive for his first story, published in the USA: $50, $100, $200 or $900?

32   In *Danny The Champion of the World*, in what did Danny live behind the petrol station?

33   In *The Witches*, to make the Grand High Witch's Formula 86, is an alarm clock: thrown into a cauldron, roasted in an oven or hung from the ceiling?

34   In *Fantastic Mr Fox*, how many men did the farmers round up to hunt down the foxes: over 50, over 100 or over 200?

35   In *Danny The Champion of the World*, who taught the seven and eight-year-olds at Danny's school: Miss Birdseye, Mr Corrado or Mr Snoddy?

36   How many boys got stuck on the tree when Mr Twit covered the branches in glue: one, two, three or four?

37   In *The Emperor's New Clothes*, a servant left a fleck of dust on the king's coat. Was he: boiled alive, hung up by his hair or minced?

38   In *The Witches*, a witch turned a boy called Leif into what sea creature: a sea slug, a porpoise or a flounder fish?

39 Which of the children in *Charlie and the Chocolate Factory* had to be taken to the juicing room to have blueberry juice removed from them?

40 In *Fantastic Mr Fox*, which one of the following could not be found growing in Mr Roach's cabbage patch: cabbage, potatoes, broccoli or peas?

41 What creature does fantastic Mr Fox find in Farmer Bean's underground cider store?

42 In *Danny The Champion of the World*, how does Danny's father say pheasant should be cooked: boiled, roasted or stir-fried?

43 In *The BFG*, what object did the Queen of England pin on to Sophie's clothing?

44 In *The Minpins*, what creature can smell an animal from ten miles away: the Triple Snorted Whafflebanger, the Red-Hot Smoke-Belching Gruncher or the Fiery Doomladen Trufflehound?

45 Inside the giant peach, did James and the insects sleep: in hammocks, on the floor or in beds?

46 How many seagulls did it take to lift the giant peach out of the sea: 301, 501, 701 or 999?

47 In *The Vicar of Nibbleswicke*, who discovered
    what was wrong with the Reverend Lee?

48 What was the name of the wealthiest churchgoer
    in *The Vicar of Nibbleswicke*?

49 Which two people get married at the end of
    Esio Trot?

50 How many sharks gathered around the giant
    peach: 10 or 20, 40 or 50, 90 or 100?

QUIZ 6

1 In *Esio Trot*, what drink does Mrs Silver offer
   Mr Hoppy after helping her with her tortoise?

2 Which one of the three farmers in *Fantastic
   Mr Fox* was the cleverest: Bean, Boggis or Bunce?

3 In *Even More Revolting Recipes*, Pishlets is:
   a sort of cake, a sort of fried fish or a sort of
   pork pie?

4 In *Danny The Champion of the World*, what was
   Danny's father doing in Hazell's Wood: poaching,
   making a campsite or stealing apples?

5   Which of the insects inside the giant peach says that he is a musician: the earthworm, the grasshopper or the centipede?

6   In *Even More Revolting Recipes*, what flavour ice-cream helps make a Fizzy Lifting Drink?

7   What did Matilda's father sell for a living?

8   In *George's Marvellous Medicine*, how many brothers and sisters does George have?

9   In *The Minpins*, what is the only way that a Red-Hot Smoke-Belching Gruncher dies?

10   In *Boy*, which one of the following was not an item of school uniform at Repton School: long tail coat, straw hat, waistcoat, bow tie?

11   Mr Twit's Beard Food is a recipe from which Roald Dahl book?

12   Which of the insects that James meets inside the giant peach eats soil?

13   What is the name of the parrot in *Matilda*?

14   In *Charlie and the Great Glass Elevator*, the President's Chief Spy thinks that the elevator was arranged to get into the Space Hotel by: Mr Hilton, Mr Savoy or Mr Ritz?

15   What colour was the new door on The Grubber in *The Giraffe and the Pelly and Me*?

16   In *The BFG*, what was placed in a hole 500 feet deep?

17   In *The Twits*, who carried a stick so that she could hit things?

18   What creatures swam up to the giant peach and started taking large bites out of it?

19   What type of bird does James get to lift the giant peach out of the water?

20   Trunky the elephant stops the Enormous Crocodile from performing which one of his clever tricks: number one, two, three or four?

21   In *The Magic Finger*, what did Mr Gregg's arms turn into?

22   In *Charlie and the Chocolate Factory*, how many times a year did Charlie get a chocolate bar?

23   In *Matilda*, who does the schoolmistress blame for putting itching powder in her gym knickers: Lavender, Matilda or Hortensia?

24 Matilda's class teacher tried but failed to move her up to a higher class: true or false?

25 In which book did someone suffer from Back-to-Front Dyslexia?

26 In *The BFG*, what two colours form the stripes on the skin of a snozzcumber?

27 In *Charlie and the Great Glass Elevator*, when Grandma Georgina became really old, which ship could she remember sailing in: the Mary Rose, the Mayflower or the Ark Royal?

28 In *The BFG*, who was the chef to the Queen of England: Mr Tibbs, Monsieur Papillion or Mr Jenkins?

29 In *Charlie and the Great Glass Elevator*, how many years younger did one Wonka-Vite pill make you?

30 In which book is there a father who tells marvellous stories to his son, Danny?

31 Can you name either of Charlie's grandmothers in *Charlie and the Chocolate Factory*?

32 Can you name either of Charlie's grandfathers in *Charlie and the Chocolate Factory*?

33   In *Dirty Beasts*, the giant snail turned into what type of bird, beginning with the letter R?

34   Which creature inside the giant peach wove a sort of rope ladder?

35   In *The Minpins*, Little Billy meets the ruler of a tree in The Forest of Sin. What is this ruler's name?

36   In *The BFG*, how many feet high was the table in the giant's cave: eight feet, 10 feet, 12 feet or 15 feet?

37   In *The BFG*, wich European country is the only one that giants don't visit to eat people?

38   At the end of *James and the Giant Peach*, which creature married the Head of the Fire Department?

39   In *Boy*, Roald Dahl turned out to be good at two sports. Were they: football and cricket, fives and squash-racquets or golf and croquet?

40   In *The Witches*, what is the title of the ruler of the witches: The Grand Poobah Of The World's Witches, The Grand High Witch Of All The World or The Witch Chief Of The World?

41 In *The BFG*, what did the Queen's butlers use for the legs of the BFG's breakfast table?

42 At what time of the day was George supposed to give his grandma her medicine: seven o'clock, nine o'clock, 11 o'clock or midday?

43 In *Matilda*, what colour cotton smock did Miss Trunchbull always wear?

44 In *Boy*, Roald Dahl said he slipped a dead animal into what sort of sweets: liquorice laces, aniseed balls, gobstoppers or chocolate raisins?

45 In *Danny The Champion of the World*, were over 100 pheasants left with: the vicar's wife, the police sergeant or Doc Spencer?

46 What was the final colour of the medicine George made in the saucepan: black, brown, green or purple?

47 Whose car was scratched and covered in pheasant droppings in *Danny The Champion of the World*?

48 Which book contains nine poems all about creatures?

49 In *James and the Giant Peach*, what was the name of the great city that the peach flew over?

50 Who was the person who ran the orphanage in *The BFG*: Mrs Clonkers, Miss Conkers or Mr Cobblers?

QUIZ 7

1 In the poem *A Hand In The Bird*, who put their hand in a lady's knickers: a doctor, a vicar or a policeman?

2 In *Charlie and the Chocolate Factory*, what part of Violet Beauregarde turned a purplish-blue first?

3 In *Fantastic Mr Fox*, was Mr Fox married or not?

4 In *George's Marvellous Medicine*, pills for a certain animal should be rationed to one or two per day, otherwise the animal will rock and roll. Which animal is this?

5 What was the name of the first Minpin Billy met and talked to?

6 In *The Emperor's New Clothes*, what did the minced-up servant reappear as: margarine, cottage pie or oil?

7   In *The Witches*, what happened to the witch on the front row who argued with the Grand High Witch?

8   In *Matilda*, Hortensia the 10-year-old girl had a boil on what part of her face?

9   In *The Giraffe and the Pelly and Me*, how often do the staff of the Ladderless Window-Cleaning Company stop for tea whilst working: once, twice or never?

10   In *Danny The Champion of the World*, what colour was Mr Hazell's Rolls-Royce car: silver, black, blue or white?

11   The Ruler of India sent the BFG an animal that he had always wanted. What was it?

12   Which of the characters in *James and the Giant Peach* became Vice-President-in-Charge-of-Sales at a high-class shoe-makers?

13   In *Charlie and the Chocolate Factory*, Willy Wonka had not been seen for how many years: two, five, 10 or 25?

14   In *The Vicar of Nibbleswicke*, what cured Back-to-Front Dyslexia: walking backwards, eating oily fish or standing on your head?

15   What Charles Dickens book had the BFG used
      for 80 years to teach himself to read and write:
      Great Expectations, Oliver Twist or *Nicholas
      Nickleby*?

16   In *Fantastic Mr Fox*, what was the name of the
      woman who entered Farmer Bean's underground
      cider store?

17   In the past, Mr and Mrs Twit had been in the
      circus as: clowns, lion tamers, monkey trainers
      or trapeze artists?

18   Is the grandmother in *The Witches*, 66, 76 or 86
      years of age?

19   What was the name of the class teacher Matilda
      adored: Miss Sugar, Miss Honey, Miss Petal or
      Miss Candy?

20   Which of Charlie's grandparents helped Charlie
      and Willy Wonka dock the elevator with the
      Space Hotel?

21   Which book won the famous Whitbread Prize in
      1983: *The Witches, Matilda, Fantastic Mr Fox* or
      James and the Giant Peach?

22   What was the official title given to the BFG by
      the Queen of England?

23 In Africa, Dahl saved a servant from what deadly animal: a lion, a black mamba snake, a leopard or a black widow spider?

24 In *Charlie and the Chocolate Factory*, Willy Wonka frequently tells a child to stop arguing and mumbling. Which child is this?

25 In *Danny The Champion of the World*, what does Danny suggest are put inside raisins in order to catch pheasants?

26 What part of the Picnic Place did the Enormous Crocodile replace with himself: a bench, a table or an umbrella stand?

27 When Matilda switched hair products to get her Dad to dye his hair, what colour did his hair become: bright red, dirty silver, light green or black-and-white stripes?

28 The Vicar of Nibbleswicke's congregation was most upset by which word said backwards: park, knits or trespassers?

29 In *The Witches*, what colour was the dress worn by the ruler of all the witches?

30 In *The Witches*, the grandmother pretended to be on the telephone to the Chief of Police from which country?

31   In *Dirty Beasts*, the scorpion stung the child on what part of her body?

32   In *Matilda*, which one of the following names does Hortensia not call Miss Trunchbull: Fiery Dragon, Foul Serpent, Evil Queen or Prince of Darkness?

33   In *Charlie and the Chocolate Factory*, who badgers her rich father to get her an Oompa-Loompa?

34   What was the surname of the family who lived in the farm next to the girl's in *The Magic Finger*?

35   The Enormous Crocodile says to Muggle-Wump that as well as eating children, he eats what?

36   One of the BFG's jars contained a dream about diving to the bottom of the ocean in a barrel of squid: true or false?

37   In *The Witches*, who was the manager of the Hotel Magnificent: Mr Stringer, Mr Spring or Mr Smith?

38   Who won Willy Wonka's competition and got to own the chocolate factory?

39   Minpin children learn to fly on the backs of which bird: thrushes, robins, sparrows or wrens?

40 In *Rhyme Stew*, how many wishes did Aladdin get from the genie: one, two or three?

41 In *The Giraffe and the Pelly and Me*, the giraffe tells the Duke of Hampshire that their Business Manager is whom?

42 Which was the last book published before Dahl died: *Esio Trot*, *The Twits* or *The Magic Finger*?

43 In *Rhyme Stew*, who did the crocodile visit and frighten?

44 As a child, what did Roald Dahl like to collect: birds' eggs, stamps or medals?

45 In *James and the Giant Peach*, who flushed Miss Spider's father down the plughole: James, Aunt Sponge or Aunt Spiker?

46 In *The Witches*, what was the first name of the boy who did not realise that he was a mouse?

47 Which of the three farmers in *Fantastic Mr Fox* had the most men working on his farm: Bean, Bunce or Boggis?

48 In *Matilda*, what object does Miss Trunchbull smash over the head of Bruce Bogtrotter?

49 In *Fantastic Mr Fox*, how many children did
    Mr and Mrs Fox have?

50 In *Boy*, Roald Dahl says that prefects at Repton
    School were called: Boazers, Corkers or
    Sergeants?

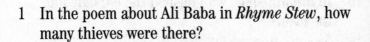

QUIZ 8

1 In the poem about Ali Baba in *Rhyme Stew*, how
   many thieves were there?

2 *Revolting Recipes* includes a recipe for Hot Ice-
   Cream for Cold Days: true or false?

3 In *Charlie and the Great Glass Elevator*, how
   many tablets did Willy Wonka give Grandma
   Georgina to bring her back to her normal age?

4 In *Dirty Beasts*, what creature pulled a lever on
   its shell to turn into a different creature?

5 Below the flying giant peach, James and the
   insects saw a great ship with a royal name. What
   was it called?

6 Roald Dahl spent all his childhood holidays on
   which island: Normsk, Tjöme, Frövik or Tranas?

7   What did the BFG blow into children's bedrooms at night?

8   After World War II, Roald Dahl lived with his mother in which English village: Uley, Great Missenden, Dursley or Pilborough?

9   In *Charlie and the Chocolate Factory*, what sort of building did Prince Pondicherry ask Willy Wonka to build entirely out of chocolate?

10 In *Rhyme Stew*, who pushed the old lady into the oven?

11 What are the name of the small people who work in Willy Wonka's chocolate factory?

12 Can you name either of the aunts James had to live with in *James and the Giant Peach*?

13 Matilda's headmistress had once been a famous: opera singer, newsreader, athlete or police-woman?

14 Fantastic Mr Fox Fry-up is a recipe in *Even More Revolting Recipes*: true or false?

15 In *The BFG*, is a snozzcumber: a type of vegetable, a type of jungle creature or a type of insect?

16   In *The Minpins*, how does the Red-Hot Smoke-Belching Gruncher like his meat: roasted, red-raw or boiled in oil?

17   In *Fantastic Mr Fox*, which food item was not present at the giant feast: hams, geese, bacon, fish?

18   In *The Vicar of Nibbleswicke*, was Arabella Prewt's house called: Shangri-La, The Haven or Dunkillin?

19   In *James and the Giant Peach*, which creature does James help take off all of its boots?

20   What sort of creature was Humpy-Rumpy in *The Enormous Crocodile*?

21   Who suggested that the Great Glass Elevator could tow the spacecraft: Grandpa Joe, Willy Wonka or Charlie?

22   In *James and the Giant Peach*, where were the grasshopper's ears: on his head, on his feet, on his tummy or on his antenna?

23   How old is Mr Twit at the start of *The Twits*: 40, 50, 60 or 99?

24   What book features the Terrible Bloodsucking Toothplucking Stonechuckling Spittler?

25   In which Dahl book does a creature cover girls with caramel and butterscotch to make them taste sweeter before he eats them?

26   In *Danny The Champion of the World*, Mr Hazell was a rich: beer-brewer, biscuit-maker or hotel landlord?

27   What is the surname of Matilda's family?

28   In *Matilda*, Miss Trunchbull took over Miss Honey's class on what day of the week?

29   In *James and the Giant Peach*, which creature inside the peach stone is proud of the fact that it is the only pest?

30   In *Matilda*, who poured half a tin of syrup onto Miss Trunchbull's chair: Lavender, Hortensia, Fred or Matilda?

31   In 1939, Roald Dahl drove 1,000km across Africa to: meet his first wife, join the military or to escape an angry landlord?

32   What was the name of Matilda's brother: Maurice, Michael or Max?

33   Roald Dahl was made Captain of Repton School when he turned 17: true or false?

34   Who faints at the sight of the BFG walking
      towards the Queen of England's bedroom: a
      cook, a gardener, a chambermaid or a security
      guard?

35   In *Danny The Champion of the World*, Danny's
      father counted how many pheasants asleep on
      the ground?

36   In *The Twits*, from what continent did both the
      monkeys and the Roly-Poly Bird come?

37   In the poem *The Emperor's New Clothes* in
      Rhyme Stew, a dozen clever men turned up the
      heating to make the King believe he was wearing
      warm, invisible clothing. What was he really
      wearing?

38   In *Matilda*, the librarian Matilda meets is called:
      Mrs Phelps, Mrs Jenkins, Mrs Page or Mrs
      Jacket?

39   Which giant in *The BFG* would dearly love to eat
      the Queen of England?

40   In *Matilda*, Miss Trunchbull threw a boy out of
      the school window for doing what in class?

41   In *Charlie and the Great Glass Elevator*, the
      Space Hotel was built by which country?

42 In which *Dirty Beasts* poem does a child have to have 100 spines pulled out of their bottom?

43 The introduction to *Esio Trot* is all about which creature?

44 In *The Witches*, who does the manager of the Hotel Magnificent have tea with: the boy's grandmother, all of the witches or Bruno Jenkins' dad?

45 What parts of the giant in *The BFG* were as big as the wheels of a truck?

46 In *Charlie and the Chocolate Factory*, Charlie's dad worked: in a toothpaste factory, as a bus conductor or as a roadsweeper?

47 What did the Vicar of Nibbleswicke say by mistake when he meant to say 'knits'?

48 In *Rhyme Stew*, Dick Whittington earned a beating from the cook by breaking: a cup, a plate or a vase?

49 In *The Vicar of Nibbleswicke*, what item did Reverend Lee attach to his forehead with an elastic band to help him walk backwards more safely?

50 In *Rhyme Stew*, what sort of creature started the race between the tortoise and the hare: an owl, a fox or a badger?

QUIZ 9

1 Which of Roald Dahl's children was hit by a taxi as a baby and had brain damage: Olivia, Tessa or Theo?

2 At the age of 22, to which continent was Roald Dahl posted as an employee of the Shell Oil Company?

3 In which book are over 80 witches turned into mice by their own magic formula?

4 After Matilda's parents flee the country, who becomes her new guardian?

5 In *The Toad and the Snail*, what country did the boy and the giant toad visit?

6 Which of the following items is not found in the Grand High Witch's Formula 86: the beak of a blabbersnitch, a part of a telescope or 20 frogs' eyes?

7   In *Esio Trot*, Mr Hoppy kept on replacing Mrs Silver's tortoise with one that was how much heavier: two ounces, four ounces or half a pound heavier?

8   In *James and the Giant Peach*, what sort of weather did James and the others first watch the Cloud-Men make: snow, hailstones or rain?

9   In *Matilda*, how much pocket money does Miss Honey get per week?

10 The first Minpin Billy saw had hair of what colour?

11 In *Charlie and the Great Glass Elevator*, really strange creatures emerged from which part of the Space Hotel?

12 In *James and the Giant Peach*, how many hundred policemen climbed up the building to get to the giant peach?

13 According to Willy Wonka, Vermicious Knids being burned up in the atmosphere create: meteorites, shooting stars or comets?

14 In *The BFG*, after the Queen of England rings the King of Sweden, does she make a phone call to: Baghdad, New York, Stockholm or Edinburgh?

15   What creature charged into the Enormous
     Crocodile when it was disguised as a tree?

16   At the end of *Charlie and the Chocolate
     Factory*, which child is left with a purple face:
     Mike Teavee, Violet Beauregarde or Augustus
     Gloop?

17   Which of the creatures in *James and the Giant
     Peach* was always looking on the gloomy side of
     things?

18   Which member of staff at Matilda's school once
     threw the hammer at the Olympic Games?

19   In *Danny The Champion of the World*, the
     pheasant-shooting season starts on the first
     day of what month?

20   What was Roald Dahl's favourite hobby whilst
     he was at Repton School: photography, stamp-
     collecting or cricket?

21   In *The Magic Finger*, Mr Gregg smashed the
     family's guns into small pieces using what tool?

22   In *Charlie and the Great Glass Elevator*, if you
     are a minus, do you spend all your time: standing
     up, sitting on a chair or lying down?

23   In *James and the Giant Peach*, how many hundred firemen stormed up the building to get to the giant peach?

24   What sort of factory did the giant peach crash through, leaving two large holes?

25   In *The Twits*, whose beard covered his face and was full of parts of old meals?

26   In *Charlie and the Great Glass Elevator*, who had to feed their father-in-law baby food: Mr Bucket, the President of the United States or Mrs Bucket?

27   Which one of the following is not an ingredient of Wonka-Vite: the snout of a proghopper, the front tail of a cockatrice or three slices of snozzcumber?

28   In *The Witches*, which one of the following was not a girl captured by witches: Birgit Svenson, Ranghild Hansen or Christian Matthias?

29   *Revolting Recipes* contains a recipe called: Fleshlumpeater's Pie: true or false?

30   In *Matilda*, what is Lavender's favourite meal at school: sausage and beans, shepherd's pie, chicken salad or pizza?

31 When Roald Dahl had a hip replacement operation, he placed the old hip bone on his writing desk: true or false?

32 What item did the ruler of the witches allow all the other witches to remove first: gloves, wigs or shoes?

33 In *The Minpins*, when Billy got older and too big to fly on the Swan, who started to visit him at his house?

34 How did Grandma carry the two mice through the hotel in *The Witches*?

35 In *Dirty Beasts*, what creature's favourite red meat is you?

36 In the poem *The Pig* in *Dirty Beasts*, which country did the pig live in?

37 In *Danny The Champion of the World*, when Danny's father fell into the pit, what did he break?

38 In *The Witches*, the witches posed as which charity organisation: the RSPCA, the RSPCC or the RSPB?

39 In which book, but not *The BFG*, does a man say that he has seen the BFG once?

40   Which book contains a recipe for Luminous
Lollies for Eating in Bed at Night?

41   What sort of food do the Gregg family first try to
eat in *The Magic Finger*?

42   How many drops of the Grand High Witch's
magic formula must the witches put in each
sweet?

43   Roald Dahl crashed an aircraft and was seriously
injured in which year: 1939, 1940, 1941 or 1942?

44   In *Danny The Champion of the World*, what was
Mr Hazell's first name?

45   What was the name of Roald Dahl's second wife:
Jacqueline, Brenda, Felicity or Hermione?

46   In *The Witches*, what are the grandmother and
the mouse going to use to kill any mouse-witches
they create?

47   In *Charlie and the Chocolate Factory*,
Willy Wonka's private yacht was made from a
hollowed-out giant boiled sweet: true or false?

48   In *The Witches*, Roald Dahl says that real
witches like to do away with how many children
per week: one, two or three?

49   Roald Dahl says in *Boy* that he was given the
     choice of two schools to attend at age 13. Can
     you name either?

50   In the poem *The Tortoise and the Hare*, which
     creature double-crossed the tortoise?

QUIZ 10

1   In *Esio Trot*, how many years had Mrs Silver had
    her tortoise: five, eight or 11?

2   In *Esio Trot*, did Mrs Silver want her pet to: grow
    bigger, eat less or stop digging up her flowers?

3   In *The BFG*, how many soldiers worked on each
    giant, tying them up with chains: four, six, 40
    or 60?

4   The Grand High Witch's blue glass bottle
    contained how many doses of her magic formula:
    100 doses, 500 doses or 1,000 doses?

5   In *Danny The Champion of the World*, how
    old was Danny when he discovered his dad was
    practising poaching?

6   Willy Wonka's lift can go sideways as well as
     up and down: true or false?

7   Which Dahl book features three wicked farmers
     called Boggis, Bunce and Bean?

8   What is the name of the author of the James
     Bond books whom Dahl met and became friends
     with during World War II?

9   In *The Giraffe and the Pelly and Me*, how did
     Billy reach the top floor of the building of the
     Ladderless Window-Cleaning Company: climbed
     up the neck of the giraffe, hopped in the
     pelican's bill or used the stairs?

10   In *The Witches*, the grandmother counted how
     many witches sitting down to dinner: 57, 84, 101
     or 200?

11   In *The Witches*, what was the name of the
     boy who was turned into a mouse as a
     demonstration?

12   Which creature in *The Giraffe and the Pelly
     and Me* was shot by the burglar's gun?

13   In *George's Marvellous Medicine*, who has a
     mouth like a dog's bottom?

14 Which spacecraft had its own gravity-making machine in *Charlie and the Great Glass Elevator*?

15 In *Even More Revolting Recipes*, puff pastry, bananas and maple syrup help make: Plushnuggets, Gumtwizzlers or Fizzwinkles?

16 In *The Witches*, what colour mouse did Bruno Jenkins turn into: a black mouse, a white mouse, a brown mouse or a striped black-and-white mouse?

17 Thanks to the efforts of Matilda, who moves into the Red House and gets her father's savings?

18 In *Danny The Champion of the World*, Danny's best friend at school is called: Sidney Morgan, Harry Chubworth or Peter Gregan?

19 In *The BFG*, what was the name of the family who ran a greengrocer's on the same street as Sophie's house?

20 How many pumps are there at the filling station in *Danny The Champion of the World*?

21 In *Rhyme Stew*, what caused the tortoise's car wheels to go flat?

22 In which book did a husband and wife get stuck standing on their heads and finally shrink away to nothing?

23 In *The Magic Finger*, who placed flowers on the graves of the dead ducks?

24 What was the name of the cow in the poem of the same name?

25 What did Mr Twit put in his wife's bed as a nasty trick: a snake, a spider, a frog or a rotten cabbage?

26 In *Charlie and the Great Glass Elevator*, what colour was the centre of a Vermicious Knid's eye?

27 In *James and the Giant Peach*, which creature made the insects' beds inside the peach stone: the centipede, the spider or the grasshopper?

28 In *Charlie and the Chocolate Factory*, which one of the following is not a rival chocolate-maker: Mr Prodnose, Mr Fickleberry or Mr Slugworth?

29 In *George's Marvellous Medicine*, who dropped a bottle of milk when they saw the giant chicken and the giant grandma?

30   In *Charlie and the Great Glass Elevator*,
     Mr Taubsypuss is a pet cat belonging to: Willy
     Wonka, Charlie Bucket or the President of the
     United States?

31   What was the name of the boy who found
     the first Golden Ticket to visit Willy Wonka's
     chocolate factory?

32   In *Boy*, what was the name of the woman who
     picked Roald Dahl out of a school identity
     parade?

33   Which of James's relatives were flattened by the
     rolling giant peach?

34   How many helicopters followed the BFG into
     giant country?

35   In *The BFG*, how many people-eating humans
     are found in giant country: six, nine, 12 or 21?

36   What is the name of the head keeper in *Danny
     The Champion of the World*?

37   In the poem *The Ant-Eater* from *Dirty Beasts*,
     what was the name of Roy's aunt: Jennifer,
     Dorothy or Millicent?

38   In *Esio Trot*, who built a mechanical gripper
     on a pole?

38 The first recipe in *Even More Revolting Recipes* is: a breakfast for growing giants, how to make frobscottle drinks or Willy Wonka's Nutcrunch Surprise?

40 In *Danny The Champion of the World*, what dried fruit do pheasants really like?

41 According to *Boy*, what is the name of the headmaster of Roald Dahl's first school: Mr Crump, Mr Coombes, Mr Harris or Mr Hardy?

42 In *Danny The Champion of the World*, what vehicle was waiting for Danny and his father after they had been poaching?

43 In *The Magic Finger*, how many ducks carried guns aimed at the Gregg family?

44 Roald Dahl joined the Royal Navy at 26 years of age: true or false?

45 What was the name of the monkey in *The Enormous Crocodile*?

46 Which *James and the Giant Peach* character ended up playing music in the New York Symphony Orchestra?

47 In *The Witches*, what injury did the mouse suffer at the hands of one of the cooks?

48 In *Matilda*, Bruce Bogtrotter is accused of stealing what food belonging to Miss Trunchbull?

49 In *Charlie and the Great Glass Elevator*, what was the name of the President's Nanny who was the Vice-President of the United States?

50 In *The Witches*, what names did the boy give his two mice: Walter and Mandy, Wendy and Michael or William and Mary?

QUIZ 11

1 Which girl in *Matilda* had a muddy pond at the bottom of her garden?

2 In *Danny The Champion of the World*, what was the name of the lady who taught the youngest class at Danny's school?

3 In *The Witches*, after the grandmother and the mouse left the Hotel Magnificent, which country did they head to?

4 In *The Magic Finger*, what did the male members of the Gregg family like to do every Saturday morning: go fishing, swimming, hunting or ride bicycles?

5   Which creature in *Fantastic Mr Fox* takes cider as medicine three times a day?

6   In *Rhyme Stew*, who did Lord Hellespont shoot by mistake in *Dick Whittington and His Cat*?

7   Roald Dahl was recruited as a spy by the intelligence forces of which country?

8   What type of everlasting sweet do Charlie and the other children see in Willy Wonka's chocolate factory?

9   Which Dahl book was published first: *The Twits*, *Fantastic Mr Fox* or *George's Marvellous Medicine*?

10   Inside the giant peach, James found a door carved into what?

11   In the Hornets Stewed in Tar recipe from *Revolting Recipes*, what sort of food takes the place of real hornets?

12   In *Charlie and the Great Glass Elevator*, how many Oompa-Loompas were there in their musical band: 10, 20 or 30?

13   What book inspired the Crispy Wasp Stings and Scrambled Dregs recipes in *Revolting Recipes*?

14   In *The Minpins*, what does Billy's mum say a
     Spittler blows out of his nose?

15   In *Esio Trot*, how many pet shops were there
     in the city where Mr Hoppy lived?

16   The Reverend Lee was hounded out of the
     parish of Nibbleswicke for speaking backwards:
     true or false?

17   In *Esio Trot*, can you remember the first name
     or the surname of the girl who became the final
     owner of Alfie the tortoise?

18   What colour button did Willy Wonka order
     Charlie to press so that the Great Glass Elevator
     could head back to Earth?

19   In *The Minpins*, what is the name of the little
     boy who becomes tired of being good and enters
     the forest?

20   What was Roald Dahl's date of birth?

21   In *Danny The Champion of the World*, how
     many pheasants were to be given to the police
     sergeant: two, four, six or 12?

22   In *James and the Giant Peach*, how many pairs
     of boots did the centipede have: 11, 21, 42 or 50?

23   In the poem *The Emperor's New Clothes*, how many times a day did the King visit his tailors: once a day, twice a day or a dozen times a day?

24   Who was the best friend of the orphan child in *The Witches*: Tommy, Sammy or Timmy?

25   In *Esio Trot*, how many tortoises did Mr Hoppy eventually buy: 10, 30, 80 or 140?

26   In *Fantastic Mr Fox*, how many boiled chickens did Farmer Boggis eat for breakfast, lunch and supper?

27   At the start of *Charlie and the Great Glass Elevator*, who grabs Mr Wonka and stops him from pressing the green button at the right moment?

28   What do giants in *The BFG* call breaking wind: whizzpoppers, snafflebangers, squeakycheeks?

29   What is the name of the child in *Charlie and the Chocolate Factory* who only watches television and does nothing else?

30   In *Esio Trot*, which creature weighs 13 ounces, a similar weight to a grapefruit?

31   What name did Dahl give his house?

32 Which character in *The Witches* was staying in hotel room number 454?

33 How many years older than Matilda was her brother?

34 What is the name of the supermodel who is Roald Dahl's granddaughter?

35 Matilda first practised her magical moving powers with which item at home: a saucepan, a pencil, a cigar or a notebook?

36 How many children did Dahl have?

37 What was the name of the teacher in *The Magic Finger* who grew whiskers and a tail?

38 In *The Giraffe and the Pelly and Me*, what is the name of the only tree that the giraffe can eat flowers from?

39 Charlie's birthday present in *Charlie and the Chocolate Factory* was a single bar of Wonka's Whipple-Scrumptious Fudgemallow Delight: true or false?

40 In the poem *The Scorpion* in *Dirty Beasts*, what colour is the scorpion's skin?

41   In *The Giraffe and the Pelly and Me*, was the giraffe male or female?

42   What is the name of the girl in *Charlie and the Chocolate Factory* who chews gum all day long?

43   In *Charlie and the Chocolate Factory*, what was the name of the amazing room which contained a river and waterfall of flowing chocolate?

44   What was the name of the witch in *The Witches* who first smelled the boy in the ballroom: Mildred, Agatha or Hildegard?

45   What creature hopes the Enormous Crocodile is caught and turned into crocodile soup: Humpy-Rumpy, Trunky or the Notsobig One?

46   What colour shoe polish did George add to his medicine for his grandma?

47   When people came to gaze at the giant peach, what did James's aunts hurry to put around it?

48   In *Esio Trot*, Mr Hoppy did what to all the tortoises in his flat: sold them, gave them away for nothing or boiled them to make tortoise soup?

49 In *Charlie and the Chocolate Factory*, how long had Violet Beauregarde been chewing the same piece of gum: three days, three weeks or three months?

50 In *Danny The Champion of the World*, who gave Danny the cane for talking in class?

QUIZ 12

1 George made a special medicine for his grandma in which room of the house?

2 In *Matilda*, who lived in a tiny farm-labourer's cottage in the woods?

3 In *Charlie and the Chocolate Factory*, Willy Wonka says that before he offered the Oompa-Loompas all the cacao beans they could eat, they were living on what insect?

4 In *The BFG*, who sat on the windowsill of the Queen's bedroom in Buckingham Palace?

5 In *Charlie and the Great Glass Elevator*, what bright colour were Willy Wonka's Wonka-Vite pills?

6 In *Revolting Recipes*, what sort of bread is used to make the body of the Enormous Crocodile?

7 In *The Minpins*, into where does Billy hope to lure the Red-Hot Smoke-Belching Gruncher?

8 In which poem in *Rhyme Stew* do the parents try to kill their own children so that there is more left for them to eat?

9 In *Dirty Beasts*, what creature does the magic toad turn into?

10 In the poem *Aladdin and the Magic Lamp* in *Rhyme Stew*, what was the name of the wicked old Chinaman?

11 In *James and the Giant Peach*, which one of the following was not found inside the peach stone: a spider, a ladybird, an earwig or a grasshopper?

12 In *The Crocodile* poem from *Dirty Beasts*, how many children does Crocky-Wock like for lunch?

13 In *Danny The Champion of the World*, what colour were the sleeping pills Doc Spencer gave to Danny's father?

14 In *Esio Trot*, what was the name of Mrs Silver's tortoise?

15   When Matilda's family thought there were
      burglars in their house, what did Matilda's father
      grab to use as a weapon: an umbrella, a golf club
      or a frying pan?

16   In *Charlie and the Great Glass Elevator*,
      which one of the following is not an ingredient of
      Wonka-Vite: a wart from a wart-hog, the hoof of a
      doppelganger, a corn from the toe of a unicorn?

17   In *Rhyme Stew*, how old was the lady in the
      poem, *A Hand in the Bird*: 16, 30, 40 or 65?

18   In *Danny The Champion of the World*, how far
      away was the nearest school: one mile, two miles
      or five miles?

19   Which one of the following was not a giant in
      The BFG: Maidmasher, Gizzardgulper or
      Livermuncher?

20   Which of Dahl's children's books was the next
      to be published after *Charlie and the
      Chocolate Factory*?

21   Where did Charlie store any bars of chocolate
      that he got: in the fridge, in a wooden box, under
      his bed or in his school bag?

22   *In Fantastic Mr Fox*, which farmer looked like a dwarf with a pot belly and had a foul temper: Bunce, Bean or Boggis?

23   In *Revolting Recipes*, the Fresh Mudburgers meal is inspired from which book: *James and the Giant Peach, The BFG* or *The Witches*?

24   According to *Boy*, who was the first to get the cane from the headmaster: Roald Dahl, Sidney Morgan or Thwaites?

25   In *The Witches*, what was the name of the hotel the boy and his grandmother take a holiday in?

26   In *Charlie and the Great Glass Elevator*, which one of Charlie's grandparents did not take Wonka-Vite pills?

27   In *Fantastic Mr Fox*, which farmer was as thin as a pencil?

28   Which one of the following was not a member of the Ladderless Window-Cleaning Company: a monkey, a squirrel, a giraffe or a pelican?

29   Which one of the following did George not put into the medicine for his grandma: shampoo, toothpaste, worming tablets or liquid paraffin?

30　In *Fantastic Mr Fox*, how many children do Mr and Mrs Weasel have?

31　In *Danny The Champion of the World*, who surprised the others by holding on to some of the pheasants?

32　In *Dirty Beasts*, what was the name of the farmer who came to feed the brainy pig?

33　What was the Enormous Crocodile's Clever Trick Number Two – acting like: a tree, a see-saw or a fairground ride?

34　In *George's Marvellous Medicine*, George tipped into his saucepan a bottle of what alcohol?

35　In *The Giraffe and the Pelly and Me*, how many floors did the building containing the Ladderless Window-Cleaning Company originally have?

36　What, according to the giant in *The BFG*, do people from Wellington in New Zealand taste of: kiwi fruit, boots, Great Danes or tomatoes?

37　What is the name of the follow-up cookbook to *Revolting Recipes*?

38　In *The BFG*, what is frobscottle: a food, an insect, a drink or a giant type of cockroach?

39   In *Charlie and the Chocolate Factory*,
     Golden Ticket winners received a supply of
     free chocolate for how long: a year, a week or
     a lifetime?

40   In *The Witches*, the mouse emptied the bottle
     of magic formula into which food?

41   Which Roald Dahl book features a boy with a
     grandma who has horrible eating habits?

42   According to Willy Wonka in *Charlie and the
     Chocolate Factory*, what type of creature
     would eat ten Oompa-Loompas for breakfast:
     a whangdoodle, a snifflewhack or a guzzlesnip?

43   Was *Charlie and the Chocolate Factory* first
     published in: the 1960s, the 1970s or the 1980s?

44   Which Roald Dahl book tells the tale of a
     grandma who grew and grew and grew?

45   In which Roald Dahl book do you first meet
     Veruca Salt?

46   In *Charlie and the Great Glass Elevator*, what
     machine does Willy Wonka say runs on sugar
     power: his yacht, the glass lift or his limousine
     car?

47   In the poem *The Cow* in *Dirty Beasts*, what did
     Daisy drop on the rude man's head?

48   What was the name of the place in *Charlie and
     the Great Glass Elevator* where Charlie and Willy
     Wonka go to add years on Charlie's relatives?

49   In *The Witches*, what sort of soup was served for
     dinner at the Hotel Magnificent: lentil and ham,
     green pea or oxtail?

50   When the chicken was fed with George's
     Medicine Number Two, what part of it grew
     enormously?

QUIZ 13

1   In *Charlie and the Great Glass Elevator*, what
    terrible space creature with a pointed bottom
    attacked the transport capsule: Grumblepuffs,
    Vermicious Knids or Zarkons?

2   On the day that Matilda's father sold five cars,
    how much money did he make in profit: over
    £2,000, over £4,000, over £6,000 or over £8,000?

3   In *The Witches*, which country has more witches
    than England: Norway, Switzerland or Germany?

4   How many Wonka-Vite pills were there in the bottle in *Charlie and the Great Glass Elevator*?

5   According to *Boy*, who was a feared teacher at St Peter's school: Captain Hardcastle, Captain Lancaster or Squadron Leader Jackson?

6   Which friend of Matilda's has a talkative parrot?

7   In *Esio Trot*, which lonely man lived in a small high-rise flat?

8   In *The BFG*, in which country were there no trees and only flat land?

9   Who ripped up the book called *The Red Pony*, which Matilda had borrowed from the public library?

10 How big is the BFG compared to other giants in giant country: twice as big as them, the same size as them or half the size of them?

11 In *Charlie and the Chocolate Factory*, Mr and Mrs Salt are thrown down the rubbish chute by the Oompa-Loompas: true or false?

12 Which of the following Roald Dahl books was published first: *The BFG*, *Charlie and the Great Glass Elevator* or *The Witches*?

13 In *Matilda*, what was the name of the girl that Miss Trunchbull swung round by her pigtails and then threw: Justine Froppwinkle, Amanda Tripp or Lavender Smith?

14 What is the name of the teacher of the top form in Matilda's school: Miss Trunchbull, Miss Plimsoll, Miss Chalk or Miss Honey?

15 What was the object the giant peach knocked over after rolling down the hill and before crushing two parked cars?

16 In Dahl's poem *Hey Diddle Diddle* from *Rhyme Stew*, what is the only thing that the thieves ever take?

17 In *The Giraffe and the Pelly and Me*, which creature carries all the water for window-cleaning?

18 How many chocolate bars did Charlie buy with the money he found in the snow?

19 In which park was an enormous house built for the BFG: Hyde Park, Regents Park, Windsor Park or Richmond Park?

20 In *The BFG*, does Sophie: have a wooden leg, wear glasses or have a broken arm in a sling?

21 Which Roald Dahl book is the sequel to *Boy*: *The Wonderful Story of Henry Sugar*, *Going Solo* or *The Giraffe and the Pelly and Me*?

22 *The Mildenhall Treasure* is a story found in: *Boy*, *The Wonderful Story of Henry Sugar* or *Rhyme Stew*?

23 How many people live in Charlie's house in *Charlie and the Chocolate Factory*?

24 In *Rhyme Stew*, who tried to cook and eat Hansel and Gretel: an old lady, an old man or an old fox?

25 In *Esio Trot*, who came up with a spell to make Mrs Silver's tortoise grow smaller?

26 The Green Pea Soup recipe from *Revolting Recipes* was inspired by: *The Twits*, *The Minpins* or *The Witches*?

27 In which book did Roald Dahl get a caning by his headmaster because of an incident in a sweet shop?

28 In *Fantastic Mr Fox*, which of the three farmers did not drive a mechanical digger to dig the hill away?

29 In *The Giraffe and the Pelly and Me*, how many gardeners does the Duke of Hampshire have to look after his flower beds: two, five, 10 or 25?

30 In *James and the Giant Peach*, what object did the wives of the Cloud-Men cook for their husbands' supper?

31 In *Boy*, was Tweedie a boy who: snored loudly, kept frogs or punched the headmaster on the nose?

32 In *The BFG*, what is the name of the one giant who does not eat people?

33 In *Charlie and the Great Glass Elevator*, which of Charlie's four grandparents was the only one not to think Willy Wonka was mad?

34 What sport did Roald Dahl play at St Peter's school every day?

35 In *Charlie and the Chocolate Factory*, when the lift crashed into the Bucket house, which old person fainted: Grandpa George, Grandma Georgina or Grandma Josephine?

36 What is the name of the strange old wooden house for sale in *The Giraffe and the Pelly and Me*?

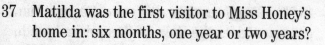

37 Matilda was the first visitor to Miss Honey's home in: six months, one year or two years?

38 In *Danny The Champion of the World*, Danny's father gives Danny's method of using sleeping pills to catch pheasants what fairy tale name?

39 In *Dirty Beasts*, what is the name of the scorpion in the poem of the same name?

40 Which object in Willy Wonka's chocolate factory is covered with rows of black push-buttons?

41 In *Charlie and the Great Glass Elevator*, which one of the following was not an astronaut: Showler, Shuckworth, Sopwith or Shanks?

42 In *The Witches*, after the mouse was spotted by the cooks in the kitchen, it hid in a sack of which vegetables?

43 In *Matilda*, who turns out to be Miss Honey's aunt?

44 In *Charlie and the Great Glass Elevator*, which of Charlie's grandparents says they once swallowed some Mexican jumping beans?

45 In *The Enormous Crocodile*, what does the Notsobig One only eat: children, fish or berries?

84

46 In *The Giraffe and the Pelly and Me*, was the Duchess of Hampshire's first name: Henrietta, Willimena, Jennifer or Cynthia?

47 In *The Giraffe and the Pelly and Me*, what company took over the building known as The Grubber?

48 Hot Frogs, Toffee Apples and George's Marvellous Medicine Chicken Soup are all recipes from which Roald Dahl book?

49 In *Dirty Beasts*, which one of the following flavourings do the French people want to add to the giant snail: parsley, basil, ginger or pepper?

50 One of the BFG's jars contained a dream of inventing a car that runs on toothpaste: true or false?

QUIZ 14

1 In *Esio Trot*, what was Mr Hoppy's job before he retired: a policeman, a zookeeper, a mechanic or a dentist?

2 Which creature in *The Giraffe and the Pelly and Me* is so hungry that it could eat a stale sardine?

3   In *Danny The Champion of the World*, what meal did Danny tell his father was his favourite: roasted pork, sausages and beans, toad-in-the-hole or fish and chips?

4   What creature in *Dirty Beasts* surprises people by sprouting wings?

5   Roald Dahl's first wife, Patricia Neal, was: a writer, a policewoman, a duchess or a film actress?

6   In *The BFG*, who suggests to the head of England's air force and army that they tie up the nine giants with chains?

7   In *The Minpins*, how does Billy leave his bedroom to go and explore the forest?

8   In *Charlie and the Great Glass Elevator*, what word did the five strange space creatures make as instructions to Charlie, Willy Wonka and the others?

9   In *Esio Trot*, can you name either of Mr Hoppy's two loves of his life?

10 In *Charlie and the Great Glass Elevator*, how many luxury bedrooms does the Space Hotel have: one, five, 20 or 500?

11   In *Fantastic Mr Fox*, which creature tunnelled into the foxes' tunnel: a mole, a badger or a vole?

12   In *The BFG*, the giant says that flowers scream if you pick them: true or false?

13   Which Roald Dahl book contains a recipe for Hair Toffee?

14   How big are the Minpins' window shutters in the trees: postage stamp-sized, napkin-sized or matchbox-sized?

15   In *Dirty Beasts*, what sort of creature ate Farmer Bland?

16   What was the name of Matilda's house: Shangri-La, The Willows, Cosy Nook or Corner Pantry?

17   In *Esio Trot*, was Mrs Silver: a lady who had never been married, a widow or married to a judge?

18   In *Boy*, Dahl says it took how many days for his family to travel from Britain to Norway?

19   Who invented Three-Course Chewing Gum?

20   What object did Mr Tibbs, the Queen's butler, give the BFG to use as a spoon?

21 In *The Vicar of Nibbleswicke*, whose dog did the Reverend Lee call 'god'?

22 In *The Witches*, what colour is a witch's spit?

23 How old is George in *George's Marvellous Medicine*: six, seven, eight or nine?

24 In *Matilda*, whose hat did Matilda cover in superglue for a trick?

25 In which book would you find a Space Hotel and Vermicious Knids spelling out words with their bodies?

26 In *Charlie and the Chocolate Factory*, who owns the largest chocolate factory in the world?

27 In *Fantastic Mr Fox*, what did the woman who entered the underground cider store carry in her hand: a knife, a rolling-pin or a shotgun?

28 *Mdisho of the Mwanumwezi* is a story from which Roald Dahl book: *Going Solo, Boy, Rhyme Stew* or *George's Marvellous Medicine*?

29 Who did the Grand High Witch gave samples of her magic formula to: the youngest witches, her favourite witches or the oldest witches?

30   In *Matilda*, how much of the cake had Bruce Bogtrotter eaten when he gave an enormous belch: a quarter, a third or half?

31   In *The Magic Finger*, what creature had the Gregg family hunted which caused the girl to get cross and put her magic finger on them?

32   In *The Witches*, when Bruno first visits the grandma's room, what fruit does he start to eat?

33   What had Mr and Mrs Twit gone out to buy when they returned to find their living room upside-down?

34   What was the name of Roald Dahl's first born child: Tessa, Olivia or Theo?

35   In *The Twits*, what bird handed the monkeys the keys to their cage?

36   How did the three farmers first try to kill fantastic Mr Fox?

37   Who visited Billy every night to take him away to visit the Minpins and other magical places?

38   In *Charlie and the Chocolate Factory*, how old were all of Charlie's grandparents: over 70, over 80 or over 90 years of age?

39 In *Matilda*, who does Miss Trunchbull blame for the reptile in her water jug: Matilda, Hortensia or Lavender?

40 In *The Giraffe and the Pelly and Me*, which Duke is the richest man in England?

41 In *Dirty Beasts*, how old was Roy's aunt: 53, 63, 73 or 83 years of age?

42 In *Matilda*, what is the name of the tall, narrow cupboard that Miss Trunchbull puts naughty children in?

43 In *The Magic Finger*, which of the girl's fingers is the magic one: her little finger, her forefinger, her middle finger or her thumb?

44 Which character had a glass eye in *The Twits*?

45 Which of the following is not a recipe in *Revolting Recipes*: Hansel and Gretel Spare Ribs, Bruce Bogtrotter's Cake, Doc Spencer's Pheasant Pie?

46 Which child in *Charlie and the Chocolate Factory* falls into the river of chocolate?

47 How many windows does Mr and Mrs Twit's house have: none, one, 10 or 100?

48 Which one of the following children was not a member of Matilda's school class: Lavender, Nigel or Prudence?

49 Did the monkeys and birds in *The Twits* cover the floor, walls or ceiling with glue?

50 How old was the Reverend Lee when he became the Vicar of Nibbleswicke?

QUIZ 15

1 Which one of Charlie's family accompanied him to Willy Wonka's chocolate factory?

2 What book inspired the Eatable Marshmallow Pillows recipe in *Revolting Recipes*?

3 According to *Charlie and the Great Glass Elevator*, which one of these is not an ingredient in Vita-Wonk: the tail of a 207-year-old giant rat from Tibet, the teeth of a 101-year-old shark or the whiskers of a 36-year-old cat?

4 According to *Rhyme Stew*, which one of the following did Aladdin help with writing stories: William Shakespeare, Jane Austen or JK Rowling?

5   What award-winning Dahl novel was published in the same year as *Dirty Beasts*?

6   What book inspired the Frobscottle recipe in *Revolting Recipes*?

7   In *Charlie and the Chocolate Factory*, what type of business did Veruca Salt's very rich father have: a building business, a peanut business or a car-making business?

8   In *The BFG*, which direction do the bubbles in giants' drinks go: up, down or sideways?

9   What sort of long black item of clothing was the giant wearing in *The BFG*?

10 In *The Witches*, what do clean children smell like to witches: dog droppings, rotten cabbage or tapioca pudding?

11 In *The Witches*, what type of animal does the Jenkins family have at their home: a cat, a goldfish or a pair of dogs?

12 Who was the deputy head of the school in *Matilda*: Mr Trilby, Miss Jackson or Mr Dawes?

13 At the start of *The BFG*, Sophie can see the giant holding what musical instrument?

14 In *The Twits*, who dreamed of becoming the owner of the first great upside-down monkey circus in the world?

15 In *The Witches*, the home of the Grand High Witch was in England, Norway, America or France?

16 In *James and the Giant Peach*, what was the name of the strange wispy creatures in the sky?

17 In *Matilda*, how many adults were needed to carry the fainting Miss Trunchbull to the sick room?

18 In *The Magic Finger*, what did the Gregg family change their name to?

19 In Willy Wonka's chocolate factory, a small hole runs between the Testing Room and what other room?

20 Which one of the following poems is from *Rhyme Stew*: *A Hand in the Bird*, *The Lion* or *The Toad and the Snail*?

21 In *The Giraffe and the Pelly and Me*, what sort of sweet did Billy give the Duke: Mint Jujubes, Scarlet Scorchdroppers or Gumglotters?

22 At the end of *Charlie and the Chocolate Factory*, which child is much thinner than before: Augustus Gloop, Veruca Salt or Violet Beauregarde?

23 What do the Minpins use as vehicles to get them about the forest?

24 In *The Giraffe and the Pelly and Me*, which creature uses a cloth to clean the windows?

25 In *Dirty Beasts*, how much did the dentist's work of pulling out the porcupine quills cost: 10, 20 or 50 guineas?

26 In *Danny The Champion of the World*, what was the name of the baby in the pram: Sidney, Christopher or Stanley?

27 In *The Witches*, how can you detect a real witch: because they are bald, because they have red eyes or because they always speak with a stutter?

28 In *Charlie and the Chocolate Factory*, what sort of toy did Mike Teavee carry lots of?

29 In *The Witches*, what was the name of the city where Grandmamma lived: Stockholm, Oslo, Edinburgh or Berlin?

30 How often did Roald Dahl write to his mother until her death: once a week, once a month or once every two months?

31 In *The Giraffe and the Pelly and Me*, what had the Duchess of Hampshire been 55 years earlier: a famous cowgirl, a crime detective, an opera singer or a cook?

32 Mrs Twit baked a bird pie on what day of the week: Monday, Wednesday or Friday?

33 In which Roald Dahl book would you read about Butcher Boy, Manhugger and a plan to send a dream to the Queen of England?

34 In the poem *The Cow* in *Dirty Beasts*, from which country did the rude man come: Iran, Afghanistan, France or Spain?

35 In *Matilda*, who orders Nigel Hicks to stand in the corner on one leg, as a punishment for being dirty?

36 In *Charlie and the Chocolate Factory*, how many beds were there in Charlie's house?

37 In *The BFG*, human beings from which country taste of hats: Turkey, France, Panama or Morocco?

38   In *Revolting Recipes*, what is used to make the green skin of the Enormous Crocodile: spinach, food colouring or cucumber slices?

39   In *George's Marvellous Medicine*, which creature did George feed his medicine to after his grandma?

40   What is contained in all the jars in the BFG's cave?

41   In *Boy*, what was the title of the woman who terrified the children at St Peter's School?

42   What do the Minpins wear on their feet to help them get around the trees of the forest?

43   In the poem *The Porcupine* from *Dirty Beasts*, what was the name of the dentist?

44   What did the school cook in Matilda bring out for Bruce Bogtrotter: a giant chocolate cake, a mountain of broccoli or a bowl of cabbage soup?

45   In *The Magic Finger*, when Mr Gregg discovered he had wings, did he get out of: bed, the bath or his armchair?

46   In *James and the Giant Peach*, which creature played music on its body that sounded like a violin?

47   Which child was thrown down the rubbish chute by squirrels in *Charlie and the Chocolate Factory*?

48   What was the name of the Reverend in *The Vicar of Nibbleswicke*?

49   Who paid a week's pocket money to borrow Fred's parrot to play a trick on her parents: Matilda, Violet Beauregarde or Veruca Salt?

50   Where did the giant in *The BFG* take Sophie after he plucked her from her bed?

QUIZ 16

1   In the poem *Aladdin and the Magic Lamp* in *Rhyme Stew*, the cave containing the magic lamp was outside which Chinese city?

2   In *The BFG*, what were the imprisoned giants to be fed on: nettles, snozzcumbers, bean soup or frobscottle?

3   In *The Giraffe and the Pelly and Me*, what was the first item that Billy saw thrown out of the window: a kitchen sink, a bathtub or a toilet?

4   In *The Witches*, what creature did the witch want to give the boy as a present?

5   In *Fantastic Mr Fox*, which family had five children: the Rabbits, the Badgers or the Foxes?

6   In *Charlie and the Great Glass Elevator*, what happened to the Oompa-Loompa during test 132?

7   In *The Vicar of Nibbleswicke*, what animal is said to commonly suffer from Back-to-Front Dyslexia?

8   In *Rhyme Stew*, who killed Lord Hellespont with his sword?

9   In *Danny The Champion of the World* there is a teacher with the nickname, Lankers. What is the teacher's proper name?

10   In *Charlie and the Great Glass Elevator*, what job did Lancelot R. Gillgrass have?

11   In the poem *St Ives* from *Rhyme Stew*, how many wives did the man have?

12   Roald Dahl died in 1990. Was he 54, 64 or 74 years of age?

13   What object did Matilda control to write on the blackboard?

14   In *Charlie and the Great Glass Elevator*, according to the President's Chief Cook, what sweet do men from Mars eat?

15   In *The Witches*, how many trunks of fake English money did the Grand High Witch have with her?

16   Which one of the following is not a giant in *The BFG*: Manhugger, Childchewer, Gristlegobbler or Bonecruncher?

17   In *Fantastic Mr Fox*, the foxes and the badger take carrots from Farmer Bunce's store for which creatures?

18   What was the name of the largest of the four monkeys that Mr Twit kept?

19   In the *Ali Baba* poem from *Rhyme Stew*, what two words did one of the forty thieves shout in order to open the rock face?

20   What does the BFG use to catch dreams?

21   In *The Magic Finger*, the girl's magic finger was on which hand?

22 In *Rhyme Stew*, was the race between the hare and the tortoise: a draw, a victory for the tortoise or a victory for the hare?

23 In *Charlie and the Chocolate Factory*, which nine-year-old child was incredibly fat: Augustus Gloop, Veruca Salt or Charlie Bucket?

24 In *Revolting Recipes*, what vegetable is used as the basis of the Snozzcumber recipe?

25 What was the first room that Charlie and the others saw after stepping out of the Great Glass Elevator?

26 How much did the child in the poem *The Porcupine*, receive as pocket money: 10p, 50p, £1 or £5?

27 *Matilda* is set in what part of England: the south-east, the Midlands, the north-west or the north-east?

28 Roald Dahl was awarded a royal honour, but he turned it down. Was this: an OBE, a knighthood or an MBE?

29 Which Roald Dahl book is subtitled *Tales of Childhood*?

30 In *Fantastic Mr Fox*, what did Farmer Bunce farm: ducks and geese, turnips, chickens or sheep?

31 In *Matilda*, which teacher taught Matilda's class how to spell the word 'difficulty'?

32 In *Danny The Champion of the World*, Enoch Samways is: the village doctor, taxi driver, police sergeant or head gamekeeper?

33 Roald Dahl won prizes from the Royal Photographic Society when he was 18 years old: true or false?

34 Which character in *James and the Giant Peach* was used to light the torch in the Statue of Liberty?

35 In *Esio Trot*, who pretends a Bedouin tribesman told him the secret to make creatures grow?

36 In *George's Marvellous Medicine*, which two of the following things did Grandma not like to eat: beetles, biscuits, slugs, caterpillars or jam?

37 In *Danny The Champion of the World*, how many pheasants were in each of Danny and his father's flour sacks: 30, 40, 50 or 60?

38   The Grand High Witch orders all the other witches to resign their jobs and buy what sort of shop?

39   Can you name either of the Mr and Mrs Gregg's sons in *The Magic Finger*?

40   In *George's Marvellous Medicine*, who suggests they build a marvellous medicine-making factory: George's mother, George's father, or George's grandma?

41   How many Minpins has the Gruncher eaten: dozens, hundreds or thousands?

42   In *The Magic Finger*, what did Philip and William Gregg feed the birds: corn, barley or bread?

43   Bunce's Doughnuts is a recipe inspired by a character in which Roald Dahl book?

44   Which creature fell off the giant peach and into the sea?

45   In *Danny The Champion of the World*, which one of the following items did Danny's Dad not make for him: stilts, a fire-balloon, a boomerang or a cricket bat?

46 In *Revolting Recipes*, what type of pasta forms a wormy meal inspired by the book, *The Twits*?

47 In *Charlie and the Chocolate Factory*, how much did a woman offer Charlie for his Golden Ticket in the sweet shop: £100, £200, £1,000 or £2,000?

48 The Toad-in-the-Hole recipe in *Even More Revolting Recipes* was inspired by which Dahl book?

49 What is the first word written on the blackboard by Matilda's piece of chalk?

50 Which book inspired the recipe, Grobswitchy Cake: *The Twits, The BFG* or *James and the Giant Peach*?

QUIZ 17

1 In *Boy*, if a teacher gave you a stripe, did it mean you were: rewarded for good homework, thrashed by the headmaster for being bad or were made into a prefect?

2 In *The Enormous Crocodile*, what was the name of Mary's brother: Timmy, Toto or Trevor?

3   In *The Giraffe and the Pelly and Me*, who helped the Duke of Hampshire turn The Grubber back into a marvellous sweet shop?

4   In *The Enormous Crocodile*, what is the favourite food of the Roly-Poly Bird: berries, nuts or birdseed?

5   At the end of *Danny The Champion of the World*, what electric-powered item was Danny's father planning to buy?

6   According to Roald Dahl in *Boy*, good and bad behaviour was rewarded with stars and stripes at which school?

7   In *Charlie and the Great Glass Elevator*, where does the President of the United States think that Charlie, Willy Wonka and the others are from: China and Japan, Mars and Venus or France and Belgium?

8   What country did Roald Dahl always go on holiday to, between the ages of four and 17?

9   In *Charlie and the Great Glass Elevator*, what is the name of the planet which is 18,427 million miles away?

10   In *Danny the Champion of the World*, how many
     pheasants did Danny and his father hope to
     poach: 50, 100, 200 or 400?

11   The Enormous Crocodile's Clever Trick
     Number Three saw him pretend to be part of:
     a fairground ride, a tree or a park bench?

12   In the poem, *Physical Training*, was the name
     of the lady gym instructor: Miss Vault, Miss
     McPhee or Miss Takenidentity?

13   What piece of furniture was inside the Great
     Glass Elevator along with Willy Wonka, Charlie
     and his family?

14   How much did James's aunts charge visitors to
     view the giant peach: one penny, one shilling or
     one pound?

15   What does Willy Wonka call the minty-sugar
     grass in his factory: traft, swudge, crimp or
     bazoom?

16   What book of poems was published in 1982, the
     same year as *The BFG*?

17   What insect does the BFG say is one of the
     biggest chatterboxes of all: earwigs, caterpillars
     or ants?

18   What nationality was the grandmother in
      The Witches: French, Norwegian or Swedish?

19   What part of his body did fantastic Mr Fox lose
      to the farmers' guns?

20   Did George feed his Medicine Number Three to:
      a goat, a cockerel, a hen or a horse?

21   In whose beer mug did Mrs Twit place a glass
      eye as a horrid trick?

22   Which James Bond movie did Roald Dahl write
      the screenplay for: *Dr No, Casino Royale* or
      You Only Live Twice?

23   Which one of the following is not a sweet at
      Willy Wonka's chocolate factory: marshmallow
      cars, square sweets which look round or sugar-
      coated pencils for sucking?

24   In *The Giraffe and the Pelly and Me*, What fish
      is Pelly the pelican's favourite: pilchard, salmon,
      cod or herring?

25   In *James and the Giant Peach*, the seagulls take
      the peach to which country?

26   In *Charlie and the Chocolate Factory*, what is
      Charlie's surname?

27 What item in Buckingham Palace did the BFG smash into, causing it to shatter when it hit the floor?

28 In *The BFG*, what was the name of the giant who ate a piece of snozzcumber containing Sophie but spat it out?

29 In the poem *The Porcupine*, what day of the week did the child get his pocket money?

30 Which one of the following was not part of George's medicine for his grandma: scouring powder, antifreeze, canary seed or hot chilli sauce?

31 In *Danny The Champion of the World*, Danny's father fell into a pit in which wood?

32 In *Boy*, what dead animal did the children put in a sweet jar?

33 Whose idea was it to stick the carpet on the ceiling of the Twits' house: the Roly-Poly Bird, Mrs Twit or Muggle-Wump?

34 What sort of vehicle pulled Grandma out of the Krankys' farmhouse in *George's Marvellous Medicine*?

35   In which book was a wife tied to balloons by her wicked husband and allowed to fly away?

36   In *Danny The Champion of the World*, what was the name of the doctor who came to treat Danny's father's injured leg?

37   What was the snake-like name of the burglar captured in *The Giraffe and the Pelly and Me*?

38   What bird warned the children away from the fairground ride on which the Enormous Crocodile was hiding?

39   What did the boy in *The Witches* catch Bruno Jenkins burning with a magnifying glass at the Hotel Magnificent?

40   In *Dirty Beasts*, what does Crocky-Wock cover boys in to make them taste better?

41   In *The BFG*, what do giants call people: popple, human dreams, sticky dolls or human beans?

42   In *The Magic Finger*, what creature took over Mr and Mrs Gregg's house?

43   Willy Wonka has a long grey beard and wears a monocle: true or false?

44 In the poem *The Emperor's New Clothes* from *Rhyme Stew*, how long did it take for the King to be frozen solid: half an hour, an hour, two hours or four hours?

45 In *Matilda*, who did Rupert Entwistle live next door to: Mr and Mrs Wormwood, Lavender or Hortensia?

46 In *Danny The Champion of the World*, who pushed the pram carrying the pheasants that Danny and his father had poached: Mrs Clipstone, Miss Birdseye or Mrs Snoddy?

47 In *The Giraffe and the Pelly and Me*, what colour was the Duchess of Hampshire's hair?

48 In *Matilda*, what is Miss Trunchbull's first name: Dorothy, Agatha or Mary?

49 In *The Minpins*, what fell into the lake causing it to boil?

50 What is the first name of Matilda's class teacher: Joan, Jenny or Jackie?

QUIZ 18

1 In *Even More Revolting Recipes*, the Hot Noodles recipe is jokingly said to be from what dog?

2 How did the girl in *The Magic Finger* mistakenly spell c-a-t in her lessons at school?

3 In *The BFG*, what is the name of the only human that the giants are afraid of?

4 In *The BFG*, to which country did the people-eating giants go the night before they visited England: Chile, Sweden, Norway or Panama?

5 In *Charlie and the Great Glass Elevator*, how many Wonka-Vite pills did the three grandparents each take?

6 In *Fantastic Mr Fox*, which farmer stuffed doughnuts with goose-liver pâté?

7 Which creature in *Rhyme Stew* had a tiny but fast car hidden underneath him so that he could win a race?

8 What body of water does the giant peach land in: a lake, the sea or a river?

9 In *Danny The Champion of the World*, was Danny's dad: a mechanic, a doctor, a factory worker or a window cleaner?

10 The Grand High Witch's Formula 86 includes
   what part of 45 brown mice: the tails, noses or
   whiskers?

11 In *The BFG*, who finally tied up Fleshlumpeater?

12 Before Roald Dahl started writing children's
   stories, what type of books did he write: horror
   and murder stories, books on law, sports reports
   or romance novels?

13 In *Esio Trot*, who worked as a mechanic at the
   bus garage before retiring?

14 How long do most giants in *The BFG* tend to
   sleep for: 40 winks, 50 winks, five hours or
   40 hours?

15 In *The BFG*, the Bonecrunching giant eats
   humans from which country?

16 According to Dahl in *The Witches*, what item of
   clothing do real witches always wear even when
   it is hot?

17 In *Esio Trot*, how often did Mr Hoppy change
   tortoises: every day, every week, every fortnight
   or every month?

18 In what month of the year do Charlie and the other winners visit Willy Wonka's chocolate factory?

19 In *The Twits*, what was the name of the bird who came to England on holiday and talked to the monkeys?

20 In *The Witches*, what knitted item did the mouse sit in as he was lowered to the Grand High Witch's balcony?

21 What sort of object covered the walls of the giant's cave in *The BFG*?

22 In *The Minpins*, the Red-Hot Smoke-Belching Gruncher cannot see in front of him, can see a short distance or can see up to ten miles?

23 In *Danny The Champion of the World*, what sort of pie did Doc Spencer's wife bring Danny: apple, cold meat, blackberry or fish?

24 Which member of staff at Matilda's school bought a car from Mr Wormwood?

25 What was the name of the headmaster of Danny's school in *Danny The Champion of the World*?

26   In *The Witches*, how many doses are there in the bottle of Mouse-Maker formula that the mouse steals?

27   Which of the farmers in *Fantastic Mr Fox* drank gallons of strong cider: Boggis, Bean or Bunce?

28   In *Danny The Champion of the World*, who had their leg in plaster for much of the book?

29   In *George's Marvellous Medicine*, was George's surname: Muddler, Kranky, Fiddler or Plough?

30   In *The Witches*, who does the boy and Bruno Jenkins go to visit straight after they have been turned into mice?

31   Which character in *Danny The Champion of the World* used to catch trout by tickling them?

32   In *Charlie and the Chocolate Factory*, what did Charlie's dad do to earn money after he lost his job in the factory?

33   What silver object did the grandmother in *The Witches* use as a bath for the mouse?

34   What was the last farmyard animal George gave his magical medicine to?

35 In which Roald Dahl book would you find a recipe for Boiled Slobbages?

36 In *The Witches*, what creature did the boy see when he entered the Grand High Witch's hotel room?

37 In *Danny The Champion of the World*, from what object did the sleeping-pill drugged pheasants start to emerge: a pram, a caravan or a Rolls Royce car?

38 In *Danny The Champion of the World*, who made the special extra-large poacher's model of a pram?

39 In *Charlie and the Chocolate Factory*, for how many years had Grandma Josephine been lying in her bed?

40 In which room in Willy Wonka's chocolate factory would you find squirrels?

41 In *Charlie and the Great Glass Elevator*, what dangerous creature can be found in Minusland: Snozzwhistles, giants, Gnoolies or Pigglegripes?

42 What did Charlie and Willy Wonka see Oompa-Loompas mining for: rock candy, peppermint crystals or golden sugar?

43 In *Danny The Champion of the World*, did Danny and his father enter Hazell's Wood to go poaching just before: sunrise, midday, sunset or midnight?

44 In which book do monkeys and birds turn two terrible people upside-down?

45 Who led the procession celebrating James and the giant peach: the mayor, the chief of police or James and the insects?

46 What book inspired the Boggis's Chickens recipe in *Revolting Recipes*?

47 *The Giraffe and the Pelly and Me* inspired which one of the following recipes: Butter Gumballs, Green Crystals or A Plate of Soil with Engine Oil?

48 What is the name of the young boy in *The Giraffe and the Pelly and Me*?

49 What room does Willy Wonka say is the most important in his entire chocolate factory?

50 In the poem *Dick Whittington and His Cat* from *Rhyme Stew*, who became a pantry boy for Lord and Lady Hellespont?

1 How many pounds did Roald Dahl pay for the motorbike which he hid at school: £18, £80 or £800?

2 Which adult in *Matilda* hates small people?

3 In *The Magic Finger*, what creature congratulated the Gregg family on their first attempt at building a nest?

4 What sort of vehicle did Roald Dahl secretly own and keep in his last year at boarding school?

5 What was the name of the Grand High Witch's latest magic formula to be used on children?

6 What was the name of Roald Dahl's boarding school as a teenager: Harrow, Repton or Eton?

7 In *Going Solo*, what does Dahl say is the Swahili word for a lion: Sahamba, Simba or Sanubo?

8 In *Danny The Champion of the World*, what was the first name of Danny's father?

9 Which farmer smells so much that fantastic Mr Fox can smell him from a mile away?

10 In *The Witches*, at what time did the witches come to collect their bottles of mouse-making formula: six o'clock, eight o'clock or 10 o'clock?

11 According to Mr Hoppy in *Esio Trot*, tortoises can live for: 30 years, 60 years or 100 years?

12 What colour was Mr Hazell's car in *Danny The Champion of the World*: black, gold, white or silver?

13 Supermodel Sophie Dahl wrote her own fairy tale in 2002: true or false?

14 What colour was the sock that the grandmother in *The Witches* lowered down the mouse in?

15 What was the first name of Sergeant Samways in *Danny The Champion of the World*: Harold, Enoch, Vincent or Arthur?

16 In the foreword to *Esio Trot*, Roald Dahl says that tortoises used to come from the northern part of which continent?

17 In *The Witches*, what colour was the soup that the mouse poured the magic potion into?

18 In *James and the Giant Peach*, how many black spots did the ladybird have on its body?

19 What is the name of the strange vegetable in *The BFG* which Sophie says tastes like frog-skins?

20 What is the name of the charity set up by Dahl's widow to help children with their health and literacy?

21 What word did the numberplate of Mr Hazell's car spell out: STOAT, BEER or JAM?

22 In *Esio Trot*, in which month of the year did the tortoise hibernate?

23 In *Charlie and the Great Glass Elevator*, which grandparent was sprayed three times with Vita-Wonk?

24 In *The Witches* what item in the Mouse-Maker formula was roasted and helped create the time delay effect?

25 Which one of the following was not a recipe in *Revolting Recipes*: Farmer Bean's Casserole, Frobscottle or Mr Twit's Beard?

26 In which hand did Mrs Twit carry a walking stick?

27 How many Oompa-Loompas did Willy Wonka test his Three-Course Chewing Gum on: five, 10, 20 or 50?

28 Who sang a long song to introduce all the giant peach's travellers to the people of New York?

29 In *Boy*, what animal droppings did young Roald Dahl put in a man's pipe?

30 What sort of fruit tree grew behind Danny and his father's caravan in *Danny The Champion of the World*?

31 In *Esio Trot*, who filled Alfie the tortoise's little house with dry hay?

32 Which Roald Dahl book ends with the main character sitting down to write the book of his adventures?

33 In which Roald Dahl book did Willy Wonka fire retro-rockets to land back in his factory?

34 What colour were the pet mice in *The Witches*?

35 In which book did the main character's father screw toothpaste caps on tubes until the factory was closed?

36 In which book would you find a wife who puts her glass eye into her husband's glass of beer?

37 In which book did Roald Dahl describe his school matron as a female ogre?

38 How old was Alfie the tortoise at the end of *Esio Trot*?

55

33

33

39 Can you name either of the shortest poems in
    Rhyme Stew?

40 In *Danny The Champion of the World*, what sort
    of toy did Danny's father warn Danny never to fly
    alone: a fire balloon, a remote-controlled aircraft
    or a kite?

41 In *The Witches*, were the witches to have tea
    with the hotel manager in: the Grand Ballroom,
    the Sunshine Terrace or the Red Lounge?

42 What colour were Wonka-Vite pills in *Charlie
    and the Great Glass Elevator*?

43 What is the name of the father monkey in
    The Twits: Roly-Poly, Muggle-Wump, Mickey
    or Ralfario?

44 Which one of the following is not found in
    Revolting Recipes: Krokan Ice-Scream, Tortoise
    on Toast or Wormy Spaghetti?

45 In which book would you find Mr Stringer, who
    worked as a hotel manager?

46 What is the name of the Mrs Clipstone's son in
    Danny The Champion of the World?

47 Which Dahl book ends with three farmers sitting
    in the rain above a hole in the ground?

48   In the *Ali Baba* poem in *Rhyme Stew*, what
     was the bearded man doing in his hotel room:
     fishing, sleeping, eating or riding a horse?

49   In *Esio Trot*, the lady who kept Alfie the tortoise,
     had how many children: one, two, three or none?

50   In which Roald Dahl book would you find an
     orphan girl called Sophie?

DEVILISHLY DIFFICULT

1 Shortly before his death, Dahl bid from his bed in an auction for a painting by which painter?

2 In *The Twits*, what was the brand of glue Mr Twit used to coat branches in order to catch birds?

3 In *The Witches*, behind which item does the mouse hide straight after entering the hotel's kitchen?

4 What was the other word for a genie used in the *Rhyme Stew* poem, *Aladdin and the Magic Lamp*?

5 What was the name of Sophie Dahl's fairy tale book, published in 2002?

6 What sort of aircraft was Dahl flying for the RAF when he was shot down, crashed and seriously injured?

7 In *The Witches*, how many seconds does the Grand High Witch's formula take to shrink and turn a child into a mouse?

8 In the poem *The Emperor's New Clothes*, what was the name of the Royal Tailor who worked in Saville Row?

9 *The Boy Who Talked with Animals* was a story from which Roald Dahl book?

10 What was the name of the Queen of England's chambermaid in *The BFG*?

11 What was the name of the girl who nearly rode on the Enormous Crocodile when he was posing as a fairground ride?

12 In *James and the Giant Peach*, what is James's full three-worded name?

13 What was Dahl's nickname amongst the other pilots he trained with in the RAF?

14 In *The Giraffe and the Pelly and Me*, for how many years had the Duke of Hampshire not been able to see out of his windows?

15 Roald Dahl's book, *Over To You* was a collection of what type of stories: flying stories, sailing stories or animal stories?

16 In which of Dahl's books would you find a Mr Killy Kranky?

17 How fast did Daisy the flying cow dive down to bomb the rude man in the poem *The Cow*, in *Dirty Beasts*?

18 *The Green Mamba* is a story from which Roald Dahl book?

19 In *The Magic Finger*, how many ducks did the Greggs successfully shoot, the weekend after the girl had put her magic finger on them?

20 In which European country in 1941 did Dahl rejoin his squadron after six months in hospital?

21 In *James and the Giant Peach*, what was the name of the woman who lost the skin off the tip of her nose: Hermione Spiker, Daisy Entwistle or Wendy Johnson?

22 In the poem *The Porcupine* from *Dirty Beasts*, what sort of chocolates did the child buy?

23 What was the name of the bottle of perfume George tipped into his saucepan of medicine?

24 The aircraft which cut the strings in *James and the Giant Peach* was flying from New York to where?

25 In *The Minpins*, what bird acts as a messenger from Don Mini to a swan?

26 In which guidebook for children did Roald Dahl tell a tale about a boy who went to the toilet in his father's sailor's hat?

27 Which two creatures in *James and the Giant Peach* set up a factory producing rope for tightrope walkers?

28 How old was Roald Dahl when he was asked to visit Hollywood by Disney, who were interested in making a film of his first children's book?

29 Roald Dahl's first wife, Patricia Neal, won an Oscar in which film starring Paul Newman: *Hud, One Flew Over The Cuckoo's Nest* or *In The Heat of the Night*?

30 In the poem *Dick Whittington and His Cat*, what was the name of the footman Lady Hellespont was caught kissing?

31 Thwaites is the son of a doctor and is found in which of the following Roald Dahl books: *The BFG, The Witches, Boy* or *Fantastic Mr Fox*?

32 In *Rhyme Stew*, which one of the following was not a creature that Aladdin feared might be in the cave: a Hippogriff, a Dragonvole, a Doodlewhang or a Boodlesniff?

33 In *Dirty Beasts*, near what bay in the United States did the family in *The Ant-Eater* poem live?

34 In *Dirty Beasts*, what creature was bought for 50,000 gold rupees?

35 In *Dirty Beasts*, how old was Miss Milky Daisy when she came to live with the narrator of the poem *The Cow*?

36 In *The Vicar of Nibbleswicke*, for whom were the ladies knitting sweaters?

37 In *The Enormous Crocodile*, what was the creature the wicked crocodile meets straight after the monkey?

38 Which of Roald Dahl's books was voted by the readers of *The Times* newspaper as the most popular children's book of all time?

39 In *George's Marvellous Medicine*, the bottle containing around 500 purple pills was for what animal?

40 What three words were on the button that Willy Wonka pressed in his glass lift when it contained him, Charlie and Grandpa Joe?

41 In *Fantastic Mr Fox*, where did the foxes' tunnel take them to first?

42 In *George's Marvellous Medicine*, was the bottle of thick yellowish liquid for: cows, chickens or pigs?

43 Can you name both of the vitamins not in Willy Wonka's supervitamin chocolate?

44 In which book was a man found to be smoking goat tobacco: *Fantastic Mr Fox*, *Boy* or *George's Marvellous Medicine*?

45 Which of the five children in *Charlie and the Chocolate Factory* is considered a bad nut by the squirrels?

46 If you spotted a woman with larger than average nostrils and clawed fingers, what might she be?

47 What sort of clothing did the King have the pretend cloth made into in the poem *The Emperor's New Clothes* in *Rhyme Stew*?

48 During World War II, Dahl was sent as a diplomat to which American city?

49 In *Boy*, what did a schoolboy called Wragg sprinkle on the floor to warn of Matron's arrival?

50 Which of the characters in *James and the Giant Peach* went on to advertise face-creams on television?

ECCENTRICALLY EASY ANSWERS

1   Charlie
2   *Matilda*
3   Big Friendly Giant
4   A man
5   *Charlie and the Chocolate Factory*
6   *The Enormous Crocodile*
7   A bird
8   *James and the Giant Peach*
9   Willy Wonka
10 *Rhyme Stew*

11 Norway
12 *The Minpins*
13 Gene Wilder
14 *Tales of the Unexpected*
15 *The Witches*
16 *Fantastic Mr Fox*
17 *Revolting Recipes*
18 Wales
19 Sophie
20 Both his mother and his father

21 Fleshlumpeater
22 An only child
23 Insects
24 Certain flowers
25 World War II
26 Mice

27 The Queen of England
28 A garden shed
29 *The Witches*
30 *The Twits*

31 *Charlie and the Great Glass Elevator*
32 True
33 Tortoise
34 *George's Marvellous Medicine*
35 *The Vicar of Nibbleswicke*
36 A hare
37 Golden
38 *Danny The Champion of the World*
39 *Rhyme Stew*
40 *Chitty Chitty Bang Bang*

41 *James and the Giant Peach*
42 An elephant
43 *Charlie and the Great Glass Elevator*
44 *The BFG*
45 In space
46 The school headmistress
47 *Dirty Beasts*
48 True
49 Two
50 *James and the Giant Peach*

MADCAP & MUDDLESOME MEDIUM ANSWERS

1	The glow-worm	26	The earthworm
2	A fighter pilot	27	*Matilda*
3	The centipede	28	A newt
4	Its tail	29	Apples
5	False	30	A 50-pence piece
6	Grandpa Joe		
7	Green	31	A pair of shoes
8	Candy Insects	32	Three
9	Clawsizzlers	33	A tunnel
10	A quiet shy man	34	At school
		35	Reinscorched steel
11	Grandma	36	Minus two
12	Crocky-Wock	37	Her eyes
13	Lavender	38	An old man
14	Six	39	Mice
15	Eight o'clock	40	Knee
16	Soak them in water		
17	24 feet	41	A treehouse
18	Inside the mattress	42	Central Park
19	Gobwangles	43	Willy Wonka
20	Saturday	44	A goat
		45	30 years
21	Sunday	46	Miss Trunchbull's
22	Their heads	47	A glass of water
23	A farmer	48	Runt
24	Five and a half	49	Magnus
25	Children	50	A swan

QUIZ 2

1	Roy	26	St Peter's
2	False	27	None
3	Bread sauce, chipped pota-	28	At night
	toes, boiled parsnips	29	Miss Honey
4	London	30	Dahl's Chickens
5	New York		
6	A football	31	James
7	The potting shed	32	Two
8	Play bingo	33	Quentin Blake
9	A mackerel	34	Liquorice
10	10 years	35	300
		36	The Ritz
11	A lion	37	The fairground
12	Miss Hansen	38	Eight
13	Frothblowers	39	The Inventing Room
14	India	40	The chocolate factory
15	Mrs Silver		
16	A thumb	41	Measles
17	The ballroom	42	Four
18	True	43	677
19	Violet Beauregarde	44	Mrs Spring
20	A doctor	45	*The Giraffe and the Pelly and Me*
21	Africa	46	The boy's room
22	Cabbage leaves	47	Five
23	The centipede	48	Tom Young
24	A type of chocolate	49	Barely damaged it
25	False	50	*Esio Trot*

QUIZ 3

1	The Forest of Sin	25	You grow older
2	Cherries	26	Blue
3	Fleshlumpeater	27	The BFG
4	Four	28	Red
5	Eric Ink	29	Its neck
6	Fizzy Lifting Drink	30	Miss Trunchbull
7	The Lobster		
8	A camel	31	Australia
9	Philip	32	Willy Wonka
10	Atlantic Ocean	33	Mr Gloop
		34	Ratitis
11	Four	35	The grasshopper
12	The Empire State Building	36	Soapo
13	A giant toad	37	Llandaff
14	Ducks	38	*James and the Giant Peach*
15	Mrs Gregg	39	*The Magic Finger*
16	Muggle-Wump	40	Mr Gregg
17	Breakfast		
18	The spider and the silkworm	41	Miss Twerp
19	The highest tree branch	42	A treehouse
20	The tortoise	43	Five
		44	Nine
21	The pig	45	Robin
22	Rope	46	Nine
23	Jack Frost	47	Trunky
24	Sofie	48	Six
		49	Willy Wonka
		50	One

QUIZ 4

1 Engineering

2 Green

3 Nuts to you

4 True

5 Earthworm, silkworm, glow-worm

6 *Even More Revolting Recipes*

7 Tomato soup, roast beef, blueberry

8 True

9 The Duchess of Hampshire's

10 A coconut tree

11 Purple

12 Nuts

13 False

14 Grandmother

15 *James and the Giant Peach*

16 The President of the United States

17 *The Vicar of Nibbleswicke*

18 False

19 Trunky (an elephant)

20 Fleshlumpeating Giant

21 Railway safety

22 Harry

23 Spain

24 20 yen

25 The kitchen

26 358

27 Every week

28 His father

29 Mrs Pratchett

30 Farmer Bean

31 Tractors with mechanical diggers

32 Mike Teavee

33 A lion and a dragon

34 False

35 Vermes

36 Two times table

37 A sweet shop

38 Mr Snoddy

39 Wonka-Vite

40 It was closed

41 *Even More Revolting Recipes*

42 'Look who's here'

43 A rhinoceros

44 Georgina

45 Anti-freeze, oil

46 Very hot

47 William

48 Veruca Salt

49 Wales

50 Sherbet Slurpers

QUIZ 5

1	All the countries of the world	24	The Bishop of Chester
2	Mary	25	Swahili
3	Knitting	26	One ton
4	A top hat	27	Aunt Dorothy
5	True	28	The Royal Air Force
6	False	29	Its tail
7	*The Lion, the Witch and the Wardrobe*	30	A helicopter
8	*The Giraffe and the Pelly and Me*	31	$900
9	On a bike	32	A caravan
10	Crows	33	Roasted in an oven
		34	Over 100
11	*The Gremlins*	35	Mr Corrado
12	An orphanage	36	Four
13	*The Twits*	37	Boiled alive
14	A high-rise flat	38	A porpoise
15	Oompa-Loompas	39	Violet Beauregarde
16	Crocodiles	40	Broccoli
17	Tortoise number eight	41	A rat
18	Breadcrumbs	42	Roasted
19	Farmer Boggis	43	A brooch
20	Sophie	44	Smoke-Belching Gruncher
		45	In hammocks
21	Wellington	46	501
22	The ladybird and the grasshopper	47	The local doctor
23	The Duke of Hampshire	48	Arabella Prewt
		49	Mr Hoppy and Mrs Silver
		50	90 or 100

QUIZ 6

1	A cup of tea	27	The Mayflower
2	Bean	28	Monsieur Papillion
3	A sort of cake	29	20 years
4	Poaching	30	*Danny The Champion of the World*
5	The grasshopper		
6	Vanilla		
7	Second-hand cars	31	Josephine, Georgina
8	None	32	Joe, George
9	If it falls into deep water	33	Roly-Poly Bird
10	Bow tie	34	The spider
		35	Don Mini
11	*Revolting Recipes*	36	12 feet
12	The earthworm	37	Greece
13	Chopper	38	The ladybird
14	Mr Hilton	39	Fives and squash-racquets
15	Red	40	The Grand High Witch Of All The World
16	The giants		
17	Mrs Twit		
18	Sharks	41	Grandfather clocks
19	Seagulls	42	11 o'clock
20	Number four	43	Brown
		44	Gobstoppers
21	Wings	45	The vicar's wife
22	Once	46	Brown
23	Hortensia	47	Mr Hazell's
24	True	48	*Dirty Beasts*
25	*The Vicar of Nibbleswicke*	49	New York
26	Black and white	50	Mrs Clonkers

QUIZ 7

1	A vicar	26	A bench
2	Her nose	27	Dirty silver
3	Yes, he was married	28	Park
4	Pigs	29	Black
5	Don Mini	30	Norway
6	Margarine		
7	She was burned to death	31	On the bottom
8	Her nose	32	Evil Queen
9	Never	33	Veruca Salt
10	Silver	34	Gregg
		35	Monkeys
11	An elephant	36	False
12	The centipede	37	Mr Stringer
13	10	38	Charlie
14	Walking backwards	39	Robins
15	*Nicholas Nickleby*	40	One
16	Mabel		
17	Monkey trainers	41	Billy
18	86 years of age	42	*Esio Trot*
19	Miss Honey	43	The dentist
20	Grandpa Joe	44	Birds' eggs
		45	Aunt Sponge
21	*The Witches*	46	Bruno
22	The Royal Dream Blower	47	Farmer Bean
23	A black mamba snake	48	A china plate
24	Mike Teavee	49	Four
25	Sleeping pills	50	Boazers

QUIZ 8

1	40	26	A beer-brewer
2	True	27	Wormwood
3	14	28	Thursday
4	The giant snail	29	The centipede
5	Queen Mary	30	Hortensia
6	Tjöme		
7	Dreams	31	Join the military
8	Great Missenden	32	Michael
9	A palace	33	False
10	Gretel	34	A chambermaid
		35	120
11	Oompa-Loompas	36	Africa
12	Aunt Spiker, Aunt Sponge	37	Nothing
13	Athlete	38	Mrs Phelps
14	False	39	Fleshlumpeater
15	A type of vegetable	40	Eating
16	Roasted		
17	Fish	41	The USA
18	The Haven	42	*The Porcupine*
19	The centipede	43	Tortoises
20	A hippopotamus	44	All of the witches
		45	His ears
21	Charlie	46	In a toothpaste factory
22	On his tummy	47	Stink
23	60	48	A cup
24	*The Minpins*	49	A rear view mirror
25	*The Enormous Crocodile*	50	A fox

QUIZ 9

1	Theo	27	Three slices of snozzcumber
2	Africa		
3	*The Witches*	28	Christian Matthias
4	Miss Honey	29	False
5	France	30	Sausage and beans
6	20 frogs' eyes		
7	Two ounces	31	True
8	Hailstones	32	Gloves
9	£1	33	The Minpins
10	White	34	In her handbag
		35	The Lion
11	The lifts	36	England
12	600	37	His ankle
13	Shooting stars	38	RSPCC
14	Baghdad	39	*Danny The Champion of the World*
15	The hippopotamus (Humpy-Rumpy)		
		40	*Even More Revolting Recipes*
16	Violet Beauregarde		
17	The earthworm		
18	Miss Trunchbull	41	Apples
19	October	42	One
20	Photography	43	1940
		44	Victor
21	A hammer	45	Felicity
22	Lying down	46	Cats
23	200	47	True
24	A chocolate factory	48	One
25	Mr Twit	49	Repton, Marlborough
26	Mr Bucket	50	The rat

QUIZ 10

1	11 years	27	The spider
2	Grow bigger	28	Mr Fickleberry
3	Six	29	George's mum
4	500 doses	30	The President of the
5	Nine		United States
6	True		
7	*Fantastic Mr Fox*	31	Augustus Gloop
8	Ian Fleming	32	Mrs Pratchett
9	Hopped in the pelican's bill	33	His two aunts
10	84	34	Nine
		35	Nine
11	Bruno Jenkins	36	Rabbets
12	The pelican	37	Dorothy
13	Grandma	38	Mr Hoppy
14	The Space Hotel	39	A breakfast for growing
15	Plushnuggets		giants
16	A brown mouse	40	Raisins
17	Miss Honey		
18	Sidney Morgan	41	Mr Coombes
19	The Goocheys	42	A taxi
20	Two	43	Three
		44	False
21	Nails	45	Muggle-Wump
22	*The Twits*	46	The grasshopper
23	Mrs Gregg	47	The end of his tail
24	Miss Milky Daisy		was cut off
25	A frog	48	A piece of chocolate cake
26	Red	49	Miss Tibbs
		50	William and Mary

QUIZ 11

1	Lavender	26	Three
2	Miss Birdseye	27	Grandma Josephine
3	Norway	28	Whizzpoppers
4	Go hunting	29	Mike Teavee
5	Badgers	30	The tortoise
6	Lady Hellespont		
7	Britain	31	Gipsy House
8	An Everlasting Gobstopper	32	The Grand High Witch
9	*Fantastic Mr Fox*	33	Five years older
10	The peach stone	34	Sophie Dahl
		35	A cigar
11	Seeds	36	Five: one boy, four girls
12	20	37	Mrs Winter
13	*James and the Giant Peach*	38	The tinkle-tinkle tree
14	Hot smoke	39	True
15	14	40	Black
16	False		
17	Roberta Squibb	41	Female
18	Yellow	42	Violet Beauregarde
19	Billy	43	The Chocolate Room
20	13 September 1916	44	Mildred
		45	Humpy-Rumpy
21	Two	46	Brown
22	21	47	A fence
23	A dozen times a day	48	Gave them away for nothing
24	Timmy	49	Three months
25	140	50	Captain Lancaster

QUIZ 12

1 The kitchen
2 Miss Honey
3 Caterpillars
4 Sophie
5 Yellow
6 A baguette
7 The lake
8 *Hansel and Gretel*
9 A giant snail
10 Jock MacFaddin

11 An earwig
12 Six
13 Red
14 Alfie
15 A golf club
16 The hoof of a doppelganger
17 40
18 Two miles
19 Livermuncher
20 *The Magic Finger*

21 In a wooden box
22 Bunce
23 *James and the Giant Peach*
24 Thwaites
25 Hotel Magnificent
26 Grandpa Joe
27 Farmer Bean

28 A squirrel
29 Worming tablets
30 Six

31 Doc Spencer
32 Farmer Bland
33 A see-saw
34 Gin
35 Three
36 Boots
37 *Even More Revolting Recipes*
38 A drink
39 A lifetime's supply
40 Soup

41 *George's Marvellous Medicine*
42 A whangdoodle
43 1960s
44 *George's Marvellous Medicine*
45 *Charlie and the Chocolate Factory*
46 The glass lift
47 A cowpat
48 Minusland
49 Green pea
50 Its legs

QUIZ 13

1	Vermicious Knids	25	Mr Hoppy
2	Over £4,000	26	*The Witches*
3	Norway	27	*Boy*
4	12	28	Boggis
5	Captain Hardcastle	29	25
6	Fred	30	Snowballs
7	Mr Hoppy	31	Snored loudly
8	Dream Country	32	The BFG
9	Matilda's father	33	Grandpa Joe
10	Half the size	34	Football
		35	Grandma Georgina
11	False	36	The Grubber
12	*Charlie and the Great Glass Elevator*	37	Two years
13	Amanda Tripp	38	The Sleeping Beauty
14	Miss Plimsoll	39	Stingaling
15	A telegraph pole	40	The lift
16	Cash		
17	The pelican	41	Sopwith
18	Two	42	Potatoes
19	Windsor Park	43	Miss Trunchbull
20	Wears glasses	44	Grandma Georgina
		45	Fish
21	*Going Solo*	46	Henrietta
22	*The Wonderful Story of Henry Sugar*	47	The Ladderless Window-Cleaning Company
23	Seven	48	*Revolting Recipes*
24	An old lady	49	Parsley
		50	True

MADCAP & MUDDLESOME ANSWERS

QUIZ 14

1 A mechanic
2 The pelican
3 Toad-in-the-hole
4 The cow
5 A film actress
6 The BFG
7 Climbs out of his window
8 Scram
9 Flowers, Mrs Silver
10 500

11 A badger
12 True
13 *Revolting Recipes*
14 Postage stamp-sized
15 The pig
16 Cosy Nook
17 Widow
18 Four
19 Willy Wonka
20 A garden spade

21 Arabella Prewt's dog
22 Blue
23 Eight
24 Her dad's
25 *Charlie and the Great Glass Elevator*

26 Willy Wonka
27 A rolling-pin
28 *Going Solo*
29 The oldest witches
30 Half

31 A deer
32 Bananas
33 Guns
34 Olivia
35 The Roly-Poly Bird
36 With their guns
37 Swan
38 Over 90
39 Matilda
40 The Duke of Hampshire

41 83
42 The Chokey
43 Her forefinger
44 Mrs Twit
45 Doc Spencer's Pheasant Pie
46 Augustus Gloop
47 None
48 Prudence
49 The ceiling
50 27

QUIZ 15

1 Grandpa Joe
2 *Charlie and the Chocolate Factory*
3 The teeth of a 101-year-old shark
4 William Shakespeare
5 *The Witches*
6 *The BFG*
7 A peanut business
8 Down
9 A cloak
10 Dog droppings

11 A cat
12 Mr Trilby
13 A trumpet
14 Mr Twit
15 Norway
16 Cloud-Men
17 Six
18 Egg
19 The Inventing Room
20 *A Hand in the Bird*

21 Scarlet Scorchdroppers
22 Augustus Gloop
23 Birds
24 The monkey

25 50 guineas
26 Christopher
27 Bald
28 Toy guns
29 Oslo
30 Once a week

31 Opera singer
32 Wednesday
33 *The BFG*
34 Afghanistan
35 Miss Trunchbull
36 One
37 Panama
38 Spinach
39 A chicken
40 Dreams

41 Matron
42 Suction boots
43 Mr Myers
44 A giant chocolate cake
45 Bed
46 The grasshopper
47 Veruca Salt
48 Robert Lee
49 Matilda
50 His cave

QUIZ 16

1	Shanghai	26	50p
2	Snozzcumbers	27	The south-east
3	A bathtub	28	An OBE
4	A snake	29	*Boy*
5	The Rabbits	30	Ducks and geese
6	Felt much younger		
7	Tortoises	31	Miss Honey
8	Dick Whittington	32	Police sergeant
9	Captain Lancaster	33	True
10	President of the United	34	The glow-worm
	States of America	35	Mr Hoppy
		36	Biscuits, jam
11	Seven	37	60 pheasants
12	74	38	Sweet shops
13	A piece of chalk	39	Philip, William
14	Mars Bars	40	George's father
15	Six		
16	Gristlegobbler	41	Thousands
17	Rabbits	42	Barley
18	Muggle-Wump	43	*Fantastic Mr Fox*
19	Open sesame	44	The centipede
20	A net	45	A cricket bat
		46	Spaghetti
21	Her right hand	47	£200
22	A draw	48	*Danny The Champion*
23	Augustus Gloop		*of the World*
24	Cucumbers	49	Agatha
25	The Chocolate Room	50	*The BFG*

QUIZ 17

1 Thrashed by the headmaster for being bad
2 Toto
3 Billy
4 Berries
5 An electric oven
6 St Peter's
7 Mars and Venus
8 Norway
9 Vermes
10 200

11 Part of a fairground ride
12 Miss McPhee
13 A bed
14 One shilling
15 Swudge
16 *Revolting Rhymes*
17 Caterpillars
18 Norwegian
19 His tail
20 A cockerel

21 Mr Twit
22 You Only Live Twice
23 Marshmallow cars
24 Salmon
25 America

26 Bucket
27 A glass chandelier
28 Bloodbottler
29 Saturday
30 Scouring powder

31 Hazell's Wood
32 A dead mouse
33 Muggle-Wump
34 A crane
35 *The Twits*
36 Doc Spencer
37 The Cobra
38 The Roly-Poly Bird
39 Ants
40 Mustard

41 Human beans
42 Ducks
43 False
44 Half an hour
45 Lavender
46 Mrs Clipstone
47 Red
48 Agatha
49 The Red-Hot Smoke-Belching Gruncher
50 Jenny

QUIZ 18

1	Poodles	26	500
2	Kat	27	Bean
3	Jack	28	Danny's father, William
4	Sweden	29	Kranky
5	Four each	30	The boy's grandma
6	Farmer Bunce		
7	The tortoise	31	Doc Spencer
8	The sea	32	Shovelled snow
9	A mechanic	33	A sugar basin or bowl
10	The tails	34	A goat
		35	*Even More Revolting Recipes*
11	The BFG		
12	Horror and murder stories	36	A frog
13	Mr Hoppy	37	A pram
14	50 winks	38	Danny's father
15	Turkey	39	20 years
16	Gloves	40	The Nut Room
17	Every week		
18	February	41	Gnoolies
19	Roly-Poly Bird	42	Rock candy
20	A sock	43	Sunset
		44	*The Twits*
21	Jars	45	James and the insects
22	Cannot see in front of him	46	*Fantastic Mr Fox*
23	Cold meat	47	Butter Gumballs
24	Miss Trunchbull	48	Billy
25	Mr Snoddy	49	The Inventing Room
		50	Dick Whittington

QUIZ 19

1 £18
2 Miss Trunchbull
3 The ducks
4 A motorcycle
5 Delayed Action
   Mouse-Maker
6 Repton
7 Simba
8 William
9 Farmer Bean
10 Six o'clock

11 100 years
12 Silver
13 True
14 Blue
15 Enoch
16 Africa
17 Green
18 Nine
19 Snozzcumbers
20 The Roald Dahl Foundation

21 BEER
22 November
23 Grandma Georgina
24 An alarm clock
25 Farmer Bean's Casserole

26 Her right hand
27 20
28 James
29 Goat droppings
30 An apple tree

31 Mrs Silver
32 *James and the Giant Peach*
33 *Charlie and the*
   Great Glass Elevator
34 White
35 *Charlie and the*
   Chocolate Factory
36 *The Twits*
37 *Boy*
38 30 years old
39 *Mary, Mary* and *St Ives*
40 A fire balloon

41 The Sunshine Terrace
42 Yellow
43 Muggle-Wump
44 Tortoise on Toast
45 *The Witches*
46 Christopher
47 *Fantastic Mr Fox*
48 Fishing
49 Two children
50 *The BFG*

DEVILISHLY DIFFICULT ANSWERS

1 Vincent Van Gogh.
2 Hugtight
3 A garbage bin
4 Djinn
5 *The Man With The Dancing Eyes*
6 A Gladiator
7 26 seconds
8 Mister Ho
9 *The Wonderful Story of Henry Sugar*
10 Mary

11 Jill
12 James Henry Trotter
13 Lofty
14 40
15 Flying stories
16 *George's Marvellous Medicine*
17 60 miles an hour
18 *Going Solo*
19 16
20 Greece

21 Daisy Entwistle
22 Raspberry creams
23 Flowers of Turnips
24 Chicago
25 A robin

26 Roald Dahl's Guide to Railway Safety
27 The silkworm and the spider
28 25
29 *Hud*
30 Albert Grace

31 *Boy*
32 A Dragonvole
33 San Francisco Bay
34 A giant ant-eater
35 Seven months
36 The Merchant Navy
37 The Roly-Poly Bird
38 *Charlie and the Chocolate Factory*
39 Horses
40 Up and Out

41 A chicken house
42 Cows
43 Vitamin S and Vitamin H
44 *Boy*
45 Veruca Salt
46 A witch
47 A ski suit
48 Washington D.C.
49 Sugar
50 The earthworm